Post Putin

Succession, Stability, and Russia's Future

Herman Pirchner, Jr.

ROWMAN & LITTLEFIELD
Lanham • Boulder • New York • London

Published in Association with the American Foreign Policy Council

Published by Rowman & Littlefield
An imprint of The Rowman & Littlefield Publishing Group, Inc.
4501 Forbes Boulevard, Suite 200, Lanham, Maryland 20706
www.rowman.com

6 Tinworth Street, London SE11 5AL, United Kingdom

British Library Cataloguing in Publication Information Available

Library of Congress Cataloging-in-Publication Data

ISBN 978-1-5381-3139-8 (cloth)
ISBN 978-1-5381-3140-4 (electronic)

CONTENTS

ACKNOWLEDGEMENTS 1

PREFACE 3

INTRODUCTION 5

HOW LONG WILL PUTIN RULE? 7

SUCCESSION STRUGGLES IN THE USSR AND RUSSIA 9

INSTITUTIONAL POWER IN RUSSIA 13

SCENARIOS FOR PUTIN'S EXIT 27

DOMESTIC AND FOREIGN POLICY OPTIONS
FACING RUSSIA'S NEW LEADER 33

CONCLUSION 47

ADDENDUM 49

ENDNOTES 65

ABOUT THE AUTHOR 77

APPENDIX I (SORTED BY COUNTRY) 81

APPENDIX I (SORTED BY CAUSE OF DEATH) 91

APPENDIX II 101

INDEX 111

ACKNOWLEDGEMENTS

All writers stand on the shoulders of those who taught them, either in person or through the written page. I am no exception. First and foremost, my thanks go to my wife, Elizabeth Wood, whose word-smithing and encouragement are reflected throughout this work.

Many of the basic ideas contained in these pages were developed over the course of literally hundreds of conversations with Soviet and, subsequently, Russian citizens and officials during my nearly 70 trips to the territory of the former USSR, beginning in 1989. My recent conversations with Russian citizens as well as Russian expatriates have also provided me with valuable insights into the nature and functioning of the Putin regime. But, because speculating about Putin's ability to stay in power is not a risk-free enterprise, I have chosen not to use their names.

In recent months, I greatly benefited from my discussions with many Western experts, including individuals with varying points of view from London's Chatham House and Stockholm's Institute for Security and Development Policy. Private meetings with Stephan Meister, Michael Haltzel, Stephen Blank, and Walter Zaryckyj, among others, also significantly contributed to my writing.

This work would not have been possible without a grant from the Smith Richardson Foundation, or the guidance of its Senior Vice President, Marin Strmecki, whose perceptive comments on the project's structure were especially helpful.

As writing on the manuscript progressed, the editorial and substantive comments offered by the consistently prescient Ilan Berman improved its quality. It also benefited greatly from the sharp and knowledgeable eyes of

S. Frederick Starr, E. Wayne Merry, and Borys Potapenko, among others.

Many thanks are due to Amanda Azinheira, who developed the chart (Appendix I) summarizing the fate of 127 authoritarian leaders, and to Sasha Rojavin, whose study of bilateral and multilateral treaties signed by both Moscow and Washington forms the basis for Appendix II.

Fact checking and sourcing for this monograph benefited from the work of Hayden Gilmore, Matthew LaFond, and James Amedeo.

Finally, while the individuals above should rightly share credit for the insights in these pages, any errors they contain are mine and mine alone.

Herman Pirchner, Jr.
Washington, DC
January 2019

PREFACE

Former U.S. Secretary of Defense Donald Rumsfeld famously mused about "known unknowns;" things we know that we do not know. In a similar vein, Prussia's Frederick the Great talked about "imponderables;" political events so complex that even the greatest minds can't see where they lead.

High on any such list would be the topics discussed in this monograph. No one can really know when or how Vladimir Putin will leave power. Nor can one really know who will arise to take his place, or what their policies will be.

This monograph, then, should be viewed not as a crystal ball but rather as an attempt to understand the variables that will ultimately determine the answers to the above questions. It is the author's hope that this framework will prove useful to those who will have to make policy decisions when Putin's rule does come to an end.

INTRODUCTION

N ow in apparent robust health, Russian President Vladimir Putin (born October 7, 1952) could keep power in Russia for another decade or more. But he will not keep power forever. A possible deterioration of Putin's health, his politically forced retirement or his assassination are among the unpredictable factors that could suddenly bring new leadership to Moscow.

If so, who would come to power in Russia and what policy changes, if any, could be expected during, and after, what may well be a lengthy power struggle?

The answer to these questions may be unknowable, but it is possible to posit some potential alternatives to Putin, the policies these individuals would likely embrace, and the benchmarks that may be used to predict which forces in Russia are likely to be ascendant.

As we learned through the rapid rise of the then largely unknown Putin, the man who follows Putin may not now be visible to us. But the power bases that any new Russian leader must assemble are.

Attaining political power in any country requires the mobilization of key institutions and the elites who either own or control them. Which institutions and which elites, of course, vary depending upon an individual country's culture and system of governance. For instance, the military leadership of the USSR played a significant role in Nikita Khrushchev's rise to power, while in the democratic U.S., active duty generals traditionally play no role in American elections.

It is the thesis of this monograph that understanding the institutional interests that will inevitably play a role in the selection of Russia's next leader is a good place to start when exploring the range of leaders and policies that may emerge after Putin is no longer in power.

Institutions can rally behind an individual because of an idea such as hereditary rule as was the case when the Romanov dynasty ruled Russia between 1613 and 1917. During this era, there was significant competition for the most senior government posts, but all appointments ultimately depended upon the blessings of the hereditary ruler. Since 1917, however, this has not been the case. Therefore, the author believes the study of pre-Soviet elites and institutions to be of limited use in answering the questions raised above.

By contrast, the power struggles of the Soviet era hold more relevant lessons for us, since a member of the Communist Party – not a member of an individual family – was destined to rule. With approximately six percent of the USSR's population holding party membership,[1] there was a path to power for a far larger number of people. That ascent could take years to play out and often involved the leadership of the USSR's major institutions (i.e., the Communist Party, the KGB, the Army, the permanent bureaucracy, etc).

Perhaps most important, we will examine the role of institutions and oligarchs in the rise of two post-Soviet presidents, Yeltsin and Putin. Of special interest are Putin's efforts to ensure that no effective opposition to his rule would come from either government institutions, such as they are, or from Russia's private sector. Those individuals and institutions repressed by Putin or in his camp today (regardless of their private feelings) are likely to be the same ones who will be heavily engaged in the selection of his successor.

The ability of the institutional and private sector elite in today's Russia to select Putin's successor will no doubt be heavily dependent upon circumstances. Unforeseeable domestic or international events may advance the cause of one of Russia's many interlocking factions, or that of another. However, the range of policy options available to different factions is to some extent knowable, and will be explored in the closing pages of this volume, as will suggested policy options for the United States.

HOW LONG WILL PUTIN RULE?

It is fair to ask if the chances of Putin losing power are sufficient to justify this work. AFPC Research Fellow and Program Officer Amanda Azinheira has created a chart (Appendix I) that summarizes the fate of 127 dictators/authoritarian heads of state who have ruled countries of 10 million or more since 1950. Statistics taken from this chart are used in the paragraphs below.

Death by natural causes

As this monograph goes to print, Vladimir Putin, at age 66, has already lived beyond the average life span of a Russian male.[2] How much longer could he be expected to live? According to World Health Organization (WHO) statistics, 10 percent of Russians his age will die during the next 10 years.[3] The comparable figure in the United States is 5 percent.[4]

A comparison with others in the study shows that 24 (19%) of the 127 dictators listed in Appendix I died of natural causes while in office. Their average age at the time of their death was 72 years, and they had served in office an average of 20 years. While Putin's lifespan may fall significantly outside of these norms because of the superior health care given to him and other members of Russia's elite, it is clear that Russia's president is at an age where another decade of life is not a given.

Assassination or Execution

The Azinheira research also shows that 27 (21 percent of dictators studied) were assassinated or executed. They had held power for an average of 12 years and had an average age of 56 years when they died.

Forced retirement

Fifty-three (42 percent) of the dictators listed in Appendix I were involuntarily forced into retirement but not killed. Of these, 31 lost power through coups launched by opponents in government and/or the military, 19 as a result of events following popular unrest, and three as the result of international intervention.

When they lost power, dictators in this category were, on average, 60 years old and had held power for an average of 13 years.

Voluntary retirement

Of course, not all dictatorships end badly. Eighteen (14 percent) of the 127 figures in Appendix I retired voluntarily and peacefully. Cuba's Fidel Castro is a notable example.

Still in power

As of this writing, eighteen (14 percent) of the dictators studied remain in power. But, eventually, all will be placed in one of the above categories. With an average age of 66, many are still going strong. Almost half have held power in their respective countries for eight years or less, yet this group's average tenure in power is 16 years because several have held power for a very long time (e.g., Cambodia's Hun Sen, at 35 years).

From the above, we can glean a notional idea of what fate might befall Russia's president. Of the 109 dictators no longer holding power at the study's conclusion, 67 (61 percent) were killed or forced out of office, and 24 (22 percent) died natural deaths. Only 18 (17 percent) retired voluntarily. These numbers are not likely to engender a feeling of security in Putin or other dictators.

SUCCESSION STRUGGLES IN THE USSR AND RUSSIA

I n all countries, those aspiring to power, and their senior political teams, study the successes and failures of those who came before them. In countries led by dictators, senior political operatives can discuss the theory and practice of making a coup or organizing the type of "color revolutions" that previously toppled governments in Georgia and Ukraine. In democracies, the senior political operatives can talk about the strengths and weaknesses of previous campaigns for President or Prime Minister. Of course, each country has its own unique circumstances, and Russia is no exception. Those wishing to replace Putin have and will continue to study how power has previously changed hands in Moscow, because employing at least some of these methods will be their path to success. Below are brief summaries of lessons learned when power changed hands in the USSR, and subsequently in post-Soviet Russia. A longer and more detailed description is provided in the Addendum. The reader may find special interest in the pages that describe the steps Putin took to consolidate his power.

How Soviet and Russian Leaders Rose to Power: Lessons Learned

When there are multiple power centers and no monopoly on the use of force, it will take a long time for the new leader to consolidate power. Following Vladimir Lenin's death in 1924, a collective leadership and more than ten years of power struggles preceded Joseph Stalin's absolute rule. Collective leadership also followed Stalin's death in 1953, and it took Nikita Khrushchev five years before his power became largely uncontested.

Following Khrushchev's overthrow in 1964, Leonid Brezhnev rose from yet another collective leadership to become the dominant Soviet figure in just two years. However, it took Brezhnev more than a decade to fully consolidate his own power. More recently, it also took Vladimir Putin more than a decade to bring oligarchs, regional officials, the media and other Russian institutions under his regime's control.

The ability, over a period of years, to place allies in positions of power can be decisive in power struggles. As General (or First) Secretaries of the Communist Party, Stalin, Khrushchev, and Brezhnev had the ability to ensure that their friends were named to key positions in the Soviet bureaucracy. Later, these friends helped their mentors rise to dominance in the USSR. No similar position exists in Putin's Russia, but the principle remains the same and several people (discussed below) are actively working to put their people in positions of power.

If the Army chooses to involve itself in a power struggle, it will be decisive, as it has the most guns. Marshall Zhukov, and Army units loyal to him, assisted Khrushchev's rise to power. Zhukov's aid was also central to Khrushchev's narrowly retaining power in 1957. The army, by then anti-Khrushchev, also played a minor role in the ultimate removal of Khrushchev in 1964. When Yeltsin's rule was challenged by forces from the Duma in 1993, he prevailed after military units shelled the Duma's headquarters. The lessons drawn from these events no doubt contributed to the decision of Yeltsin and subsequently Putin to vacation with their respective Defense Ministers.

Having a powerful mentor helps – especially one whose health/age makes it highly unlikely that he will ever become a rival. Mikhail Gorbachev was championed by long-serving Politburo member Mikhail Suslov, who died some months before Gorbachev assumed power. Vladimir Putin was promoted when Boris Yeltsin knew he did not have much longer to live.

Not all power is resident in Moscow; regional elites are important. During the 1991 coup attempt in Moscow, pro-Yeltsin forces made hundreds, if not thousands, of calls to regional leaders to rally support and send the message to the security forces, who were tapping the phones, that the country was behind Yeltsin.

"Carpe Diem," seizing the moment. Yeltsin was very good at this. When

the political balance of power was changing, he moved against his patron, Gorbachev. When it was still risky to do so, he publicly quit the Communist Party. When the coup attempt happened, he bet all. In his 1993 standoff with the Supreme Soviet, he used force to prevail. When it came time to step down in a way that protected himself and his family, he did so.

Repression can work. Stalin kept power by killing his rivals, both real and imagined. The entire country became fearful and intimidated as his purges claimed more than twenty million lives. These events were horrible beyond comprehension, but they were also effective; Stalin kept power. Khrushchev reduced the number of killings and managed to remove many fellow Politburo members. However, those who were not purged later joined new Politburo members in removing Khrushchev from power. Brezhnev's political killings and the use of gulags proved more effective; he died in office. Putin so far has operated successfully on the principle that it is not necessary to kill as many as Stalin in order to keep opponents in line. Targeted and well-publicized killings, as well as asset appropriation, will work.

In the short to medium term, loyalty can be bought. Putin and Yeltsin learned that enriching elites and permitting them to export part of their fortunes buys loyalty – at least in the short and medium term. Those with a great deal to lose are not likely to mount political challenges.

Identification with the Russian Orthodox Church provides legitimacy. The Cameralist ideas so favored by Catherine the Great hold that religious institutions, as everything else, should be an instrument of the state. In much the same vein, Putin enriched church leaders, and their praise, in turn, gave him legitimacy. At the same time, designated church leaders have advanced defenses of Russian policy at home and abroad.

Internal and external propaganda helps control the country. Soviet and Russian leaders have, with varying degrees of success, used propaganda to distract from their failures at home and abroad.

Use of force abroad can divert attention from problems at home. When serious domestic opposition ceases to exist, external aggression may prove useful in distracting the masses from focusing on problems the leader has not managed to solve. For instance, Putin's failures at home likely contributed to his 2014 decision to invade Ukraine, and the collapse of his plans to take far more of Ukrainian territory likely contributed to his decision to use military force in Syria the following year.[5]

INSTITUTIONAL POWER IN RUSSIA

All Russian institutions and elites are affected by those who govern Russia. What follows is a summary of the most important of those groups as well as some thoughts on the role they could play in any potential power struggle. We also examine what institutional or personal interests have the potential to motivate them beyond a common interest in keeping and/or getting money and/or power. Additionally, should any come into the possession of compromising political material, there will be a temptation to use it – especially since Russian society is structured in such a way that almost everyone in politics or business is guilty of something.

Of course, it is possible for individual members of Russia's elite to belong to more than one group, and therefore to have potentially conflicting interests. For instance, an FSB official could also be both an oligarch and a member of some regional elite.

The Russian Army
The Russian Army has one million standing troops and 2.6 million reservists.[6] It commands the largest stockpile of nuclear weapons in the world. However, these numbers are likely not relevant in a struggle for power. The key question will be who commands, will use, and can count on the absolute loyalty of battalions that can be brought into the streets of Moscow on short notice and with the willingness to use lethal force.

Such a commitment on the part of the Russian Army in any power struggle would be decisive. No other institution has more raw power. However, it is not a given that the Army would intervene because of the factors listed below – all of which will be part of the discussions of succession scenarios in the chapter on "Scenarios for Putin's Exit."

If the army is sharply divided for whatever reason, and one faction decided to use force to install its own people in positions of power, it could lead to a civil war that no army faction is likely to want. Therefore, a politically divided army is likely to remain neutral. However, things would be quite different if one part of the army strongly supported or opposed a candidate at the same time that the rest of the army did not feel it had a big stake in the fight.

1. Close ties between key generals and someone aspiring to the leadership of Russia may be decisive. Khrushchev's ties to the Army[7] (from his time as a military commissar) may have been crucial in his rise to power, as well as his success in overcoming the attempt to unseat him in 1957. Future contenders to power will certainly evaluate the possibilities emanating from their personal relationship with key generals – especially those commanding units near Moscow. Awareness of this problem led to Putin's 2018 establishment of a Directorate within the Russian Army responsible for ensuring the army's loyalty to his regime.[8]

2. By 1964, Khrushchev had lost favor with the Army because of funding and political issues. As a result, the generals chose to stay on the sidelines as Brezhnev (who also had Army ties from his time as a military commissar during WW II) used political means to depose Khrushchev. This lesson will not be lost on Presidential aspirants as they formulate their views on defense policy.

3. Historically, the army has been cautious about intervening in political events – often waiting until it understood who would win, or who was sure to win with its support. Witness the Army's actions in 1991, when the coup plotters successfully ordered tanks to the center of Moscow only to find that the Army was not prepared to use force and stood with Yeltsin. Understanding the tipping point between the deployment of the Russian Army and its decision to use force may one day be critical to decisions made in both Moscow and Washington.

4. If the political process is going smoothly (e.g., as was the case in the transfer of power from Yeltsin to Putin), the army will not consider becoming involved.

Possible interests unique to the Army

1. Battles over funding for hardware, salaries, and perks played a role in the overthrow of Khrushchev, and these issues are no less important to the Army today.

2. Dissenting opinions about Moscow's use, or nonuse, of force abroad or internally have the potential to motivate parts of the Army to take action.

The Military Intelligence Directorate (GRU)

The number of GRU employees and their functions is a Russian state secret. However, the agency is thought to control as many as 25,000 *Spetsnaz* troops (special forces akin to U.S. Green Berets or Seals)[9] in addition to running Russia's largest spy network.[10]

Assuming the GRU leadership did not follow the Army's lead, how could their assets be used?

1. Assassination squads could eliminate a rival or create a political crisis.
2. Even a fraction of the GRU's 25,000 Spetsnaz forces could carry the day if no other forces choose to fight against them.
3. The GRU's huge contingent of foreign spies gives it: a) the ability to collect damaging information on senior Russian officials traveling abroad – information that could be used in a leadership struggle, and b) the occasional ability to create an international incident that may benefit one of the aspirants to power.

As power struggles are inherently unpredictable and highly risky, the GRU will have a good argument to simply wait quietly for the new leader to emerge. However, the presence of GRU alumni (e.g., Vladislaw Surkov) participating in any power struggle might result in a different calculation.

Possible interests unique to the GRU

1. To varying degrees, its members would act against plans to favor the SVR and/or FSB at expense of the GRU.
2. Because of unique military knowledge, the GRU may feel the need to oppose military recklessness or incompetence.

The Foreign Intelligence Service (SVR)

As is the case with the GRU, the SVR, which is thought to have about 13,000 employees,[11] is involved in assassinations and the collection of intelligence that could be used in any competition for power. However, the SVR's lack of ability to launch a military operation likely means that it would not be a major factor in any conceivable struggle to succeed Putin.

1. To varying degrees, its members would act against plans to favor the GRU or other organizations at the expense of the SVR.
2. Because of any unique knowledge of the world it possesses, the SVR may feel the need to oppose those acting recklessly in the name of Russia.

The National Guard (Rosgvardia)

In April of 2016, Vladimir Putin formally created the National Guard of Russia, which reports directly to him via Russia's Security Council and is run by his former bodyguard, Viktor Zolotov.[12] Its estimated 340,000 troops[13] were taken from the Ministry of Internal Affairs' (MVD) OMON and SOBR divisions. OMON (Mobile Unit for Special Purposes) is the larger of the two and specializes in riot control as well as paramilitary deterrence. SOBR (Special Unit for Quick Reaction) was estimated to have around 5,000 officers in 2007.[14] It placed first among 37 countries competing in the 2015 Annual Warrior Competition held in Jordan.[15] Other competitors included the U.S. Marine Corps and China's Assault Hawk Commando Unit. The troops of both units are primarily based in major cities, have been involved in all serious political and/or armed conflicts in post-Soviet Russia, and are likely to be involved in future struggles as well.

1. Should a challenge to Putin's rule emerge, it is likely that Putin's former bodyguard will use his troops to continue to protect the current President.
2. Should Putin die, the use of the National Guard is far more difficult to predict. It has both the power to be a factor in any power struggle, and the recent tradition of using it.[16] However, absent Putin, it is not a given that the National Guard will do so, as there may be no consensus among its leadership.

Possible interests unique to the National Guard

If the Guard's top leadership is not trusted by the new President, it will be quickly replaced, even if the institution as a whole remains intact. Simply put, no authoritarian leader will permit those who are not loyal to have the primary responsibility for protecting his/her life.

Ministry of Interior Affairs (MVD)

The employees of the MVD are stationed throughout Russia. Once much bigger and more important, the MVD has diminished in stature in recent years. However, it still runs:

1. the General Administration for Traffic Safety;
2. the Federal Drug Control Service, which reportedly employs around 40,000 people.[17] With an estimated 70,000 drug-related deaths each year and many more addicted Russian citizens,[18] MVD officials undoubtedly have files on the families of officials, or those who are themselves users of narcotics and other drugs;
3. the Directorate for Migration Affairs, which oversees international passports, resident registration (to live in some cities you must be officially registered), and immigration control. The latter is a serious issue, as officials have estimated that only 3 to 5 million of the 10 and 12 million foreign workers in Russia are legally present in the country;[19] and
4. investigation of some economic crimes.

In any power struggle, the Interior Ministry will have the power to blackmail individuals throughout the government. Collecting *compromat* (compromising material that can be used to keep someone under your control) is part of what the ministry does and it is safe to say that the Ministry has amassed a lot of it. After all, it is very hard to function at a high level in Russian society without breaking some rules.

Possible interests unique to the MVD

Elements of the MVD have highly profitable working relationships with criminal organizations – especially at the regional level. They will want the *status quo* to continue. As a result, corrupt MVD officials will oppose those who would: 1) reduce their income by permitting new people to benefit from the graft; 2) arrest select MVD officers on charges of corruption; or 3) aim to significantly reduce corruption throughout the MVD.

The Federal Protection Service (FSO)

Tasked with protecting the President of Russia and other high-ranking Russian officials, the FSO employs approximately 20,000 uniformed employees (including a dedicated "Kremlin regiment") and a few thousand plain clothes officers.[20]

Apart from the firepower it can bring to any unrest, the FSO controls the secure communications system that is used by senior officials to communicate with each other. Under certain circumstances:

1. The armed forces of the FSO are the first line of defense against any potential coup or "color revolution." Their decision to remain loyal to the President, or alternatively to move against him, could be decisive.
2. Its ability to monitor the communications of senior leaders could give the FSO early knowledge of the level of support of all factions any time the future leadership of Russia is in doubt.

Possible interests unique to the FSO

1. Any successor to Putin will likely want his own person in the top two or even three tiers of the FSO's leadership, as he will need total confidence in those primary responsibility is to protect their life. The current FSO leadership understands this, and likely will look for guarantees about its future.
2. There is a chance that some of the current FSO leadership will have ties to the new President and/or his team, and will make an effort to stay or be promoted in the organization's ranks when the new President takes power.

The Federal Security Service (FSB)

The FSB, under the patronage of its former head, Vladimir Putin, has grown in size and power at the same time as both active agents and those on "active reserve" have amassed great wealth. When Putin first rose to power, the core missions of the FSB were counterintelligence, fighting organized crime, and ensuring economic and financial security.[21] Since then, Putin has strengthened his main power base by engineering the FSB's takeover of the Border Guard Service as well as the Federal Agency of Government Communication and Information (FAPSI).[22]

Throughout Russia, major economic players all have ties to the FSB, because without its cooperation it is very hard to make big money. In turn, when big money is made, individual FSB agents get their share. This economic connection makes former and current FSB agents a big part of practically all regional and local power structures, as well as those at the federal level. It also means that they will be players in any political maneuvering involved in the selection of a successor to Putin, and are more than likely to want it to be one of their own.

However, the FSB does not possess military capabilities of its own and, if things turn violent, will be dependent upon its ability to influence organizations with guns to either use force or stay on the sidelines.

The major complication lies in the FSB's lack of loyalty to any single person or cause other than Putin. He has unified them, but that does not mean they will remain unified in the event of a power struggle.

Possible interests unique to the FSB

Under Putin, senior FSB officials, at both the local and national level, have used the power of their organization to enrich themselves. Therefore they will worry about life under any new President. Will they be exposed to criminal liability? Can they keep their assets, as well as preserve their ability to continue to use the FSB's coercive power in the pursuit of more money? Pondering these questions will no doubt incentivize the FSB's leadership to prevent the rise of any leadership team with a serious anti-corruption agenda or one that wishes to make wholesale changes to those FSB personnel currently benefitting the most from corruption.

Regional elites

As the coup attempt of 1991 faltered, the views of the regional elites became progressively more important. That coup collapsed in days, in part because the regions, which collectively had deep personal/economic/political ties to key people in all important Russian institutions, did not support it. A similar dynamic may emerge if there is a serious and lengthy struggle to replace/succeed Putin. Though regional elements may simply want more autonomy (see discussion on pages 29-30), to a significant degree all regions have the following in common:

1. *Local economic interests.* Of Russia's 85 legal subdivisions (22 Republics, 9 Krais, 46 Oblasts, 3 Federal Cities, 1 Autonomous Oblast, and 4 Autonomous Okrugs), 14 of them serve as donor regions, subsidizing the remaining 71.[23] On an ongoing basis, these donors want to keep more of their own money (e.g., the percent of revenue from oil coming from their oblast) and those receiving subsidies want to get more. Additionally, most regions have their own pet projects that need help from Moscow. For instance, when the often heavily flooded areas of Siberia have a long planned dam project cancelled because of the high costs of fighting in Ukraine and/or Syria, they may look for a leader that spends more money inside of Russia.

2. *Divided loyalties of the elite.* The elite of any region may, or may

not, act in unison. If not, the reason may go beyond personal opinions. For instance, the leaders of the local FSB may feel closer to other members of the regional elite than they do to the FSB's national leadership. A local oligarch may feel closer to his region than he does to richer Moscow oligarchs with whom he does business.

Putin's Team

Putin ensures that those close to him gain political power and wealth. This is possible, in part, because Putin's resolution of disputes is accepted. Few, if any, in his core group have any interest in risking much to change the *status quo*. However, if Putin leaves office, Putin's team will cease to be a coherent force as its members scramble to resolve their inherently incompatible interests. This struggle will have winners and losers, and will not end until stability is achieved under the new President.

Political Office Holders

The person who succeeds Putin will likely: 1) be a governor or hold a major office in Moscow; 2) have been appointed with the approval of Putin; 3) either have an FSB background or be acceptable to that organization; 4) have wealth as a result of his participation in Russia's kleptocracy; 5) be under 70; and 6) be a man.

As previously stated, it is not possible to know now who this person will be. He may not yet have ascended to any visible position. Therefore, the names listed below are merely to outline the type of biography the next leader is likely to have. In light of point five above, people of different generations have been selected.

Sergei Sobyanin (born 1958) has held many senior government positions and performed well in all of them. They include service as head of Putin's Presidential Administration (Chief of Staff), Deputy Prime Minister, Governor of Tyumen Oblast, and Mayor of Moscow since 2010.

Alexi Dyumin (born 1972) has had an extensive career in the FSO, including a stint as Putin bodyguard. In 2014, working with the GRU, Dyumin oversaw the annexation of Crimea. His short tenure as Deputy Defense Minister was followed, in 2015, by his appointment to the governorship of the Tula Oblast.

Andrei Turchak (born 1975) served nine years as governor of Pskov and is currently Deputy Chairman of the Federation Council (the upper house of Russia's Parliament). He also serves as General Counsel of Vladimir Putin's ruling "United Russia" political faction.

Anton Alikhanov (born 1986), after brief periods as Deputy Chairman of the Kalingrad Regional Government and Acting Governor, was appointed Governor of Kalingrad in 2017. He previously worked in Moscow at the Ministry of Industry and Trade, as well as at the European Economic Commission.

Political Power Brokers

Whoever comes to power will need to have individual champions who can influence key people or institutions to back their candidate. Apart from Putin, whose support may be decisive in picking his own successor, the following have, with Putin's support, been especially active in getting their favorites appointed to major Russian posts in both Moscow and the provinces. In the short term, this makes these figures, as well as others doing the same thing, more powerful. In the longer run, it positions them to play a larger role in the selection of the man who will lead Russia after Putin. That this effort is underway highlights the growing realization of the elite that there will be life after Putin, and that it is time to begin preparing for it.

KGB veteran and billionaire *Yury Kovalchuk* (born in 1951) has been a close colleague of Putin's for more than 30 years, and reportedly serves as the President's personal banker. Without putting any distance between himself and Putin, Kovalchuk has also been quite successful in placing people loyal to him throughout the government, thus leaving himself in a position to play an independent role should Putin suddenly disappear from the scene.

Igor Sechin (born in 1960), bound to Putin through a common KGB background, is now the very wealthy Chief Executive Officer of state-owned oil giant Rosneft. Before assuming that post, Sechin served in several top positions with Vladimir Putin, including as his Chief of Staff when the latter was First Deputy Mayor of St. Petersburg, as Head of Prime Minister Putin's Secretariat, and as First Deputy Chief of Putin's Presidential Administration. In short, he has a long and very close relationship with the President, and has been using it to place his people in government. Among the many officials who owe their success to Sechin is Gleb Nikitin, the Governor of Nizhny Novgorod. Sechin's success in personal placement, as well as his close ties to Putin and the FSB, cause many to view him as the second most powerful man in Russia.

Sergei Chemezov (born in 1952) has been a friend of Putin's since their overlapping KGB service in East Germany. As CEO of state engineering concern Rostec, Chemezov controls 14 holding companies that jointly employ about 450,000 people – mostly in Russia's defense industries. Consistent with his hardline views and closeness to Putin, Chemezov's assets have been frozen by the EU and Rostec's access to U.S. debt markets has been limited.

Sergey Shoigu was born in 1955 of a Tuvan father who held senior Communist Party positions in the Soviet Republic of Tuva and a Russian mother who also had Soviet era credentials. After a highly successful 20 year run as Minister of Emergency Situations, he became Minister of Defense in 2012. Especially in the wake of his oversight of Russia's military operations in Syria, Shoigu's power has continued to increase. In places like Syria, Sudan, and Libya he has participated in, or taken charge of, negotiations normally reserved for the Foreign Ministry. He has also been successful in placing allies in other parts of the Russian government. While his Tuvan and non-mainstream religious background make him an unlikely candidate for President, it is apparent that Shoigu has put himself in a position to influence any succession struggle that may occur, and has taken steps to maintain and expand his power base. Sergey Shoigu is a man to watch.

Movements

Sergey Kurginyan's "Essence of Time" movement rues the dissolution of the USSR and believes that capitalism is incompatible with Russia's cultural tradition. Kurginyan, who stood with Duma leader Ruslan Khasbulatov against then-President Boris Yeltsin in 1993, claims to have structures in most major Russian cities that are capable of organizing large demonstrations should the opportunity and need arise. Whether this is true or not, Kurginyan bears watching as his activities could not be sustained without a cooperative relationship with at least some faction of the FSB.

With a claimed 2015 membership of 160,000[24] and the ability to influence many times that number, the Communist Party of Russia still has the capacity to play a role in any power struggle. While its membership is old and declining, it nonetheless has the ability to put people in the streets, should mass protests prove useful. Additionally, through their membership – some of whom serve in the Duma or elsewhere in government – the Communists have an additional ability to influence events if there is a serious contest for power.

Media

As previously noted, Putin has brought Russia's media firmly under his control. Killings, threats, and forced changes in ownership have made it increasingly difficult for any media outlet to say things critical of Putin, even though members of his government may, from time to time, be fair game. After a brief review of media in Russia, we will discuss how the media landscape could change if Putin was no longer President.

Television

For 85 percent of Russians, television serves as the main source of news.[25] Estimates of the number of active Russian TV stations run as high as 3,300. Accurate or not, such numbers create a picture of political and ideological diversity that does not actually exist. Among those who watch the daily news or weekly news roundups, the lion's share of viewership is claimed by three state owned/controlled channels: *Channel 1* (formerly *ORT*), *Rossiya 1* (formerly *RTR*), and *NTV*.[26] Four additional stations, with viewership ranging between two and five percent, are either state owned/controlled or run by the billionaire Yury Kovalchuk, who is widely recognized as "Putin's Banker." TV networks with smaller viewership are owned by the Russian military and the Russian Orthodox Church. As can be expected, both broadcast dependably pro-Putin messages.

Radio

As in many countries, most of Russia's 2,400 commercial and public radio networks have a non-stop music format. However, when it comes to news, two state-run radio networks and a third majority-owned by Gazprom dominate the fawning coverage of Putin.

The partial exception is *Ekho Moskvy*. Famous for its stance against the attempted 1991 *coup d'etat* and long viewed as an independent liberal voice by its estimated 900,000 daily listeners, Ekho Moskvy has increasingly come under state control. It is now 66 percent owned by Gazprom Media. At the same time, some of *Ekho Moskvy*'s best known journalists (such as Tatiana Felgengauer, Olga Bychkova, Maxim Kurnikov, and Alexandr Pluschev)[27] were forced to go into exile or live under threats to their lives. As a result the station's independence has been curbed considerably, and probably will become even more circumscribed in the future.

Cyberspace

As of 2017, more than 76 percent of Russia's population had access to the internet.[28] However, posting items with political content is risky. Some Russian internet bloggers have been arrested while social media apps as well as political/social content have been blocked.[29]

These instances of government control show every sign of continuing. The Russian government has begun restricting Virtual Private Networks (VPNs) and other internet proxies[30] as well as requiring private companies to share personal user data with the government.[31] Additionally, a least four separate government organizations (ROSKOMNADZOR, the Prosecutor General's Office, the Federal Service for Surveillance on Consumer Rights and Wellbeing, and the Federal Drug Control Service) have the right, under Russian law, to block content from any site.[32] Websites large enough to be classified as mass media (that is, "printed, audio and audio-visual and other messages and material intended for an unlimited range of persons") are subject to warnings that they are not adequately censoring data on their sites. A site receiving two such warnings in one calendar year runs the risk of being completely shut down. This threat, quite naturally, has led to a good amount of self-censorship on the part of news outlets and web-based media.

Self-censorship is also encouraged by physical attacks on bloggers and online journalists. Sixty-seven attacks were recorded in 2017, as compared to 49 in 2016 and 28 in 2015.[33] Topics deemed especially unfit for the web include government corruption, Ukraine, Crimea, negative comments about Putin as well as items not permitted in many other countries (such as child pornography).

Newspapers

The BBC reports the presence of over 400 daily newspapers in Russia.[34] All major national titles are Moscow-based and in the hands of the government or Putin-friendly owners. Previous newspaper owners who did not please the Kremlin voluntarily sold their properties or were forced out of business. For instance, when Mikhail Prokhorov ran into trouble with the Kremlin because one of Prokhorov's media holdings reported on Putin's family, he avoided the Kremlin's wrath by selling his media properties to Kremlin-friendly Gregory Berezkin. This is how business empires are built in Putin's Russia. As of this writing, Berezkin controls print publications whose daily circulation totals over six million – close to the combined daily circulation of the two major government-owned papers, *Rossiyskaya Gazeta* and *Argumenti I Fakti*.[35]

While most Russians get their news from television, the newspapers described above could play an important role after Putin's reign because they are read by those who will be involved in any potential power struggle.

The Role of the Media in Any Power Struggle

Under Putin, all major media outlets have more or less the same line, especially as it relates to the President. The moment he is gone, however, the authority of anyone to revise or enforce guidelines for publications will be in question. Writers and owners may test, or even ignore, existing guidelines as they seek to play a role in the evolution of Russian society. Tensions may also exist within individual media organizations – especially if the majority of writers/broadcasters have political views that differ from those of their editors and/or owners. In any case, until the new power structure is stable, there will be fights among personalities and factions. The outcome of these contests could be important, as the arguments used in the media will be developed and circulated by those engaged in any power struggle. With some modifications, the above is also true for those who produce internet content. For what outcomes will this broadly defined media community fight?

1. *Freedom of the press.* The number of Russian journalists killed since 1992 currently stands at 58.[36] The number beaten, threatened, or in voluntary exile can be assumed to be substantially higher. The number of their friends and sympathizers in the media is larger still. If a serious power struggle occurs, one can expect many media figures to support those political figures who promise the media more latitude. They will do so with the knowledge that their careers could be hurt or helped depending upon who rises in Russia's post-Putin leadership.

2. *Avoid being on the losing side.* For reasons of belief or pragmatism, others may avoid all controversial issues or actively support those who favor strict government control of the media as well as other parts of society. If the reformers win, their job will be put at risk.

Oligarchs

A 2018 British House of Commons report notes that "Contemporary oligarchs owed their wealth to the President (Putin) and act, in exchange, as a source of private finance for the Kremlin."[37] Additionally, not one is in open opposition to Putin. As long as Putin remains alive and in power, this system is stable. In other circumstances, their actions are less predictable.

In January 2018, the U.S. Treasury Department published a list of 96 Russian "oligarchs" who were worth one billion dollars or more.[38] Undeniably, they, and the hundreds of smaller oligarchs in their economic orbit, have the financial power to influence any struggle to replace Putin and his team, especially a protracted one. Most would oppose any prospective leader who wished to follow popular sentiment (given that the masses are quite anti-oligarch) and tax or take away significant parts of their fortunes. But who they might support is less clear. Oligarchs, after all, are not a coherent interest group. It is probable that many self-identify not as oligarchs, but as members of one or more other groups with which they are associated (e.g., FSB, regional elite, etc.).

Therefore, expect the oligarchs to stay neutral or be divided by their answers to two questions. First, would a prospective leader protect my assets and my ability to make more money and spend it freely abroad? Second, do I, or those I am closest to, have strong ties to anyone with a serious chance of getting the top job?

Scientists

Scientists and intellectuals have an interest in being able to control their own institutes. This was the practice under all leaders before Putin. Now, however, political operatives who syphon off funding meant for science are increasingly in control of the scientific establishment. This is publicly resented by members of the country's prestigious Academy of Sciences, who can be expected to use their influence to support any Putin successor who would return control (and autonomy) back to the Academy. The influence these scientists wield, moreover, is notable. As the national security establishment is dependent upon scientists for nuclear, rocket, and other militarily applicable technologies, the argument of these specialists that they are unable to work productively when under government/kleptocratic control will have at least some effect. The grievances of these scientists will also be taken seriously by anyone connected to the economy. $130 billion (a lot of money in Russia's meager economy) is currently on the books as a result of the sale of atomic energy plants.[39] Scientists not only design and run these plants, they also help train the technicians responsible for their day-to-day operation.

SCENARIOS FOR PUTIN'S EXIT

A t some point in the future, Putin will leave power, either voluntarily or not. Some versions of how such a transition may come to pass are explored below.

SCENARIO I: Putin Voluntarily Leaves Power

Putin is the only visible person who can keep peace among Russia's competing factions and personalities. In the words of Andrei Kolesnikov, a Senior Fellow at the Carnegie Moscow Center, "Putin remains the umbrella brand for all power groups, none of which wants to leave the shelter of the umbrella. That would mean a loss of protection."[40]

Princeton Professor Stephen Kotkin puts it another way: "Mr. Putin is no longer the arbiter over a 'scrum of competing interests,' but is, instead, the leader of a single faction that controls all the power and all the wealth. This faction needs its protector to stick around so it can stay rich – and stay alive...There is really no way for Putin to retire peacefully."[41]

As Putin, in the words of Kolesnikov, becomes more a grandfather figure than a father figure, all those under his umbrella will begin to wonder who will protect them when Putin is gone, and they will begin to hedge their bets. Putin, in turn, will begin to wonder how to protect his own money – much of which is reportedly in the names of others and invested in the West. This state of affairs is problematic if Putin loses power, as the people holding his money may no longer listen to his directions. They could simply keep the funds for themselves and/or cut a deal with the new person in power. Putin would also have to fear for his physical safety; he has made many enemies and that list may now include, for reasons just described, former friends who hold billions of his fortune in their names. The most likely ways things could play out if Putin retires follow:

1. Of the eight leaders who preceded Putin, only one (Yeltsin) left power voluntarily. It is possible that Putin would follow Yeltsin's lead and step down when he has a Prime Minister (the constitutional successor in such circumstances) who he feels can keep power as well as protect Putin's interests. But, even if well-intentioned, will that person be strong enough – with Putin's quiet help – to do both? Putin's longtime Prime Minister, Dmitri Medvedev (perhaps picked because few see him as a real replacement for Putin) is viewed as not being able to do either, much less both. This creates a problem for Putin as he may have great difficulty finding a new and durable Prime Minister he can trust. Regardless of whether he stays with Medvedev or picks someone else, there will be some danger for Putin. That reality strongly argues for Putin not to step down unless he thinks the end of his life is years, rather than decades, away.
2. Putin may "half retire" to a post that enables him to make the biggest decisions, while leaving everything else to the new President and his Prime Minister.
3. The longer Putin remains in office, the greater will be the political activity of those who wish to replace him. If Putin voluntarily steps down, Presidential aspirants will have a serious choice: to try and gain power through the electoral process – presumably running against a former Prime Minister who, according to the constitution became President – or to attempt to come to power through the use of force. No doubt someone is secretly considering these options today.

Policy Implications for the U.S.

1. American policymakers should not assume that Putin's handpicked successor would necessarily continue to follow the same policies. The new person might resemble Khrushchev, the unexpected reformer who came from Stalin's inner circle, or be an ardent nationalist who emerges from Putin's inner circle.
2. It could take years for the new President's personal power to be fully consolidated. During that time, provocative Russian behavior toward other countries will likely lessen or stop altogether. This will give the countries in Russia's Near Abroad time to strengthen their economic and diplomatic positions.
3. If Putin "half retires," it would mean that he could also, at some point, unretire.

4. If Putin's policies are perpetuated and/or someone with strong nationalist views comes to power, more aggressive Russian behavior in Kazakhstan and other parts of the former Soviet Union will become more likely.

SCENARIO II: Putin Involuntarily Leaves Power

The transition of power in any authoritarian state is inherently unstable. Today's Russia is no exception. Putin's power is more personal to him than a reflection of the office that he holds. During the four years when Putin was Prime Minister and Medvedev was President, no one in Russia doubted that Putin was still in charge – even if some in the West did. Because there will likely be no obvious successor to Putin and no widely accepted rules for Putin's replacement, it is almost a given that there will be intense competition to replace him, and that this competition could become violent and/or last a number of years.

Option 1: Putin Dies of Natural Causes

If Putin sees his death coming ahead of time, things may well play out in a fashion similar to the scenario described in the section above. However, if he dies suddenly, as did Stalin, then the situation is likely to be quite different.

The Prime Minister will officially take power, but without Putin's protection may not keep it for very long. Undoubtedly, all those who aspired to post-Putin power will have their contingency plans, but how developed those will be is unclear. After all, no one would want Putin to hear about them approaching dozens of others concerning their plans to gain power.

This means there will likely be a period of uncertainty while all aspirants to power (perhaps including the former Prime Minister), and their respective teams, seek to build support among the sources of power described above. Then, if no one has a decisive advantage, their struggle may play out in one of the following ways.

1. A more or less free election could determine the next President. This choice would be built around mobilizing allies who control or heavily influence all of Russia's major political subdivisions (e.g., Oblasts, Krais, etc.). Preparation for this option has already begun. As described previously, efforts are now underway by different power centers to place loyal individuals in key bureaucratic spots, because all involved understand that winning a Russian election has two distinct elements: 1) winning the votes, and 2)

deciding who counts and reports the votes.

2.   Someone, or more likely a small group, could have their minions stage unruly demonstrations in multiple cities and then, with enough armed backing, announce over state TV and radio that their group has taken power to save Russia from chaos. If this works (that is, no one else with significant arms opposes them), it may take years for power to be consolidated and a stable political order to be established. During that time, Russia could be expected to turn inward.

3.   Two camps could claim enough armed support that blood would be spilled – possibly, but not necessarily, in large amounts. In either case, greater repression would follow and the consolidation of the victor's power would take time.

Policy implications for the U.S.

1.   Russia can be expected to partially withdraw from the world as the power of Moscow's new leadership is consolidated. This would be a relief to Ukraine and other parts of the former USSR, which are currently subject to substantial interference in their internal affairs. However, Russia's withdrawal would also bring problems to countries currently challenged by Russia, as China – and to a lesser extent the West and others – will see an opportunity to expand their influence. America should be committed to ensuring the sovereignty and promoting the economic prosperity of those states so challenged.

2.   If internal bloodletting becomes severe, the PRC may move to advance old territorial claims in the Russian Far East and Eastern Siberia. This could be done by the movement of a few million Chinese into sparsely populated regions that belonged to China before the Russian land grabs of 1858 and 1860. This option will become more probable if Taiwan (whose absorption remains China's top priority) becomes an integral part of the PRC. Additionally, ethnic minorities in some Russian regions have long sought to avoid micro-management from Moscow. In the case of the North Caucasus republics, independence could well become the preferred option. Separatist movements in parts of Siberia also bear watching – especially if they are supported by a neighboring country.

Option 2: Putin Is Assassinated

The writer believes this to be the least likely of the four scenarios. Security around Putin is good, and those within Putin's political system would be highly reluctant to launch a violent coup because they know, from their own history, how easily they could become the next members of the Russian leadership to be killed. Still, assassination is possible and we should explore how a successful assassination attempt could play out.

If no one in Russia's political elite had any advance knowledge, things may progress more or less as if Putin had unexpectedly died a natural death. The exception might be if the assassin was identified with a group hated by Russians (e.g., a Caucasus-based *jihadist*). In that case, issues of blame and retribution would likely play a bigger role in the succession struggle.

The second variant would be an assassination planned and executed by someone who wished to replace Putin and his team – essentially, a violent coup. This might play out in two ways.

1. The assassin is not caught, or, if he/she is, has no provable or even strongly suspected ties to any of the contenders to power. In this case, those behind the assassination would have made detailed post-assassination plans – plans they could immediately begin to execute. Opposing forces, on the other hand, would be slow to rally their supporters and may be faced with a *fait accompli* before they are able to do so. If things evolve in this fashion, force (beyond the actual assassination) may not be needed. If the planners favored the Prime Minister, pursuing constitutional succession would be a good option. If they did not want the PM as the next President, they might leave him in power as a caretaker before winning the Presidential election with another candidate. Or perhaps they could gain enough backing from the force ministries to bypass the Prime Minister and/or election options entirely by establishing a committee to rule Russia until order is restored.

2. There is a clear, or strongly suspected, tie between the assassin and a contender to power. If that contender had a dominant supporter among those able to deploy and use weapons, a dictatorship (with or without ritual elections) could be established. If not, different force ministries (or parts of them) could line up behind the coup plotter or his opposition. At this point, people would start to be killed with no predictable outcome in sight.

Option 3: Internal Russian Politics Force Putin to Resign

Russian oligarchs and powerbrokers may one day decide that Putin must go. Many already chafe under the weight of international sanctions, which make it harder for them to operate freely from their second and third homes in foreign (mostly Western) countries. At some point, this state of affairs could become intolerable, and cause them to make common cause with major regional figures who are likewise fed up with the President for various reasons. Many, for example, feel that questionable military spending in places like Syria and Ukraine's Donbas region has leeched funds away from their pet projects (whether in infrastructure or other domestic programs). However, it should be noted that such potentially explosive criticisms of Putin have existed for a long time without creating the critical mass of people prepared to overthrow him.

How might that change? Any successful "coup" would have to involve those who now help keep Putin in power, and would likely not be possible without the active involvement, or at a minimum the neutrality, of the force ministries. All these people have the most to lose if a coup attempt failed, and, therefore, are highly unlikely to make any serious attempt absent a major opportunity. This could occur in the aftermath of a traumatic failure in foreign affairs, or some highly emotional domestic event. In the wake of either, a unity of public opinion might induce Putin's opponents to seize the day.

If a coup is attempted, it is likely to play out in a binary fashion.

1. A successful coup would likely lead to a multi-year power struggle among the coup leaders as well as a predisposition of the new leadership to look inward until things are domestically stable. Doing this will likely involve the exile, voluntary or forced, of some Putin loyalists, as well as other forms of retribution. The more blood is spilled, the longer this process will take.

2. If the coup fails and no blood is spilled, coup plotters will likely be jailed and have their fortunes reapportioned among those who remained loyal. Those on the fringes of the coup attempt, as well as those not in favor with Putin, can be expected to go into exile. If blood is spilled, however, expect the retribution to be bloody and the prison sentences longer. Internal order will be reestablished more quickly than in the above example, and the chances of external Russian aggression (as a diversion) would be higher.

DOMESTIC AND FOREIGN POLICY OPTIONS FACING RUSSIA'S NEW LEADER

In rough terms, there are four different ways that a post-Putin Russia can evolve: 1) Putin voluntarily leaves power and is replaced by someone who governs in practically the same manner; 2) Putin voluntarily leaves power and is replaced by someone whose foreign policies lead to a lessening of tensions with the West; 3) Putin involuntarily loses power, ushering in a new government dedicated to real economic and political reform; and 4) the above options, or some combination of them, fail and a period of chaos and prolonged instability comes to Russia. A discussion of how each option might play out follows, as do some thoughts on the implications for U.S. policy.

The Putin Crowd Stays in Power

Andrei Kozyrev, a former Russian Foreign Minister (1990-1996), sees two options if the Putin crowd stays in power:

> ....Crimea, eastern Ukraine, and Syria represent the regime's excesses. It's analogous to a river that one day rises and floods. All members of the regime wanted to follow the river's course, which means anti-Western propaganda for the people, while for themselves the West is a place for living and pleasure. But the annexation of Crimea, which was absolutely unnecessary, and the adventures in eastern Ukraine and Syria resulting in serious personal sanctions led to a flood in which they can drown.[42]

For this reason, Kozyrev continues to argue that if the same cohort remains in power after Putin's departure, "a policy adjustment might take place – not a change of course, but an adjustment. Such excesses as the annexation of Crimea or a war in eastern Ukraine or Syria can be eliminated, so that members of the regime can again travel to the West and enjoy themselves."[43]

Option One – A Policy Adjustment

Under the scenario outlined by Kozyrev, Russia's foreign military adventurism would be significantly curtailed or stopped entirely. As a result, Russia's elite would regain their freedom of movement and ability to do business throughout the world. However, Russia's foreign military adventures in Ukraine and Syria correspond to two major parts of Moscow's internal propaganda – propaganda that helps keep the regime in power. The first argument is that Russia is surrounded by enemies; the second is that Putin is restoring Russian greatness and respect throughout the world.

If Russia stopped fighting in Syria and Ukraine, and toned down other military and political provocations, a change in Russia's internal propaganda would be necessary. However such a change in internal messaging might lessen confidence in, or even destabilize, the regime.

Therefore, the question in both the West and Russia will be, "How much must Russia change before its relationship with the West can be normalized?" Further complicating decisions in Moscow may be an appreciation that, without successful reform efforts, Russia will need to employ increasingly repressive policies to contain discontent at home. Kremlin leaders may also understand that repression may not work indefinitely in a society that has (through travel and the internet) information on how people live in other countries.

China

The Peoples Republic of China has long closely studied Russia and, before it, the Soviet Union. For reasons described in the "Chaos" section below, Beijing has ambitions in the Russian Far East. However, while Beijing may view Moscow's lessening of tensions with the West as a further sign of Russia's decline (as opposed to a purely tactical move), it will likely preserve the *status quo* in its relationship with Russia until Chinese leaders see a more favorable time to act decisively in Russia's Far East. For its part, Russia should also be happy not to fundamentally change its relationship with China. Greater visible military cooperation with China would complicate Moscow's goal of thawing relations with the West and pulling away from China might needlessly sour relations with Beijing.

How U.S. policy addresses this and other levels of the Sino-Russian relationship is one of the big questions U.S. policymakers must address. Obvious U.S. options range from non-involvement to doing everything possible to aggravate the existing tensions in the relationship between Russia and China.

Russia's European neighbors
The goal will be to sufficiently normalize relations with Europe to permit Russia's elite to live and freely operate there. This probably means: 1) reaching an agreement with Kyiv that will return the currently occupied areas of the Donbas region to Ukrainian sovereign control and, 2) coming into compliance with various now-violated treaties and international norms. It does not, however, mean that Moscow's strategic goals will change. These include: Eurasianist strategies to split England from Western Europe; compromising Europe's elite; and discrediting traditional European democracy, including through the funding of nationalist parties.

Treaty compliance and other international norms
Appendix II provides a summary of the most important multilateral and bilateral national security-related treaties signed by both the U.S. and Russia or its legal predecessor, the USSR. This chart, part of a treaty study conducted in 2018 by AFPC researcher Alexander Rojavin, shows that, of the 58 listed treaties, Russia can credibly be argued to be in violation of 36. Policymakers in Washington and European capitals will accordingly need to judge with how many of these treaties Russia will need to comply, and how fully, before its elites are again welcomed in the West. In this calculus, it can be expected that the current positions of Western governments will shift – perhaps substantially so – if the Kremlin begins to come into compliance with the above.

For its part, the Kremlin will adhere to international treaties and agreements in earnest only if it decides that the costs of noncompliance (measured in sanctions and international isolation) have been too high. The U.S., meanwhile, will fully normalize relations only when it concludes that Russia is operating within international norms.

Russia's Internal Empire
An easing of relations with the West would give Moscow a greater opportunity to deal with forces within Russia that seek greater autonomy or even independence. If money now spent in Syria and Ukraine finds

its way to various Russian regions, it may, indeed, buy Moscow time. However, without fundamental reforms, the day of reckoning will only be postponed, thus increasing the probability of the negative outcomes discussed in the "Chaos" section of this work.

Russia and Central Asia
An easing of tensions with the West would also permit Moscow to pay greater attention to its declining position in Central Asia, as well as to the problems emanating from that region. Special attention would be given to preventing the rise of Chinese, American, and Islamist influences, with the latter being seen as the most dangerous for Russia. America also has interests in keeping secular (e.g., non-Islamist) governments in power, and this may create some opportunities for Russian-American cooperation.

Option Two – No Policy Adjustment

China
No policy adjustment means continued, or even heightened, tensions with the West and therefore the need to preserve or enhance Russia's already solid relations with China. As the ongoing, and perhaps increased, sanctions take their toll on the Russian economy, China will understand its ability to demand more from Russia. These demands may include: the lease of large tracts of land in Russia's Far East; more sophisticated military technology; lower prices on Russian raw materials; and diverting the flow of Russian rivers to water-poor China. These will not be easy concessions for Russia to make, however, and if it does not do so Beijing may come to view reconciliation with the West as a more attractive option.

Russia's European neighbors
Russian programs to influence domestic politics in European countries have had some success to date. For instance, they are at least partially responsible for the recent rise of European nationalist parties that favor better relations with Moscow, notwithstanding Russia's rogue behavior. However, Russia's violations of treaties, agreements, and commonly acceptable international practices have also hardened anti-Russia attitudes among most governments. As a result, sanctions against Russia not only remain in place but have been expanded. Moscow may feel that because Russians are tougher and are willing to suffer to a greater degree, France,

Germany and other countries will eventually bend to Moscow's will. The counter argument is that Western resolve will continue to increase pressure on Russia – pressure that will lead to a change of behavior, if not the regime itself.

Treaty compliance and other international norms

A Russian decision not to modify its international behavior means that the West will continue to see ongoing territorial aggression, as well as saber rattling – including unannounced flights of military aircraft into the air defense zones of Sweden and other countries, nuclear threats, continued violations of treaties and agreements, and so forth. Until Russia is willing to substantially curb the part of its behavior that is clearly outside of international norms, there is no chance of reconciliation with the West. If there is no change in Russian behavior, the West will, and should, increase and expand the pressure it puts on Moscow.

Russia's internal empire

Western sanctions, as well as the costs of ongoing military adventures, will make it harder for Russia to control the aspirations of its regions for greater autonomy or independence. The toll of Western sanctions, as well as the cost of military adventures in Ukraine, Syria, and perhaps other theaters in the future, will limit Moscow's ability to use financial incentives to mollify its domestic population. As a result, greater repression may become increasingly necessary to control those with dissenting views. Repression often works, but – as mentioned above – it alone is not likely to control separatist forces indefinitely. Should Moscow come to view regional unrest as increasingly unmanageable, Russia will feel an increased need to normalize relations with the West. The U.S. and its Western partners will also grapple with the trade-off between a perceived need to keep Russia stable and a willingness to let Russia's internal problems build if Russia does not return into compliance with international norms.

Russia and Central Asia

Failure to improve relations with the West will mean Moscow has less economic flexibility to keep pace with its geopolitical competitors in Central Asia. During this time of Russian weakness, cash-flush China, Western countries, and other actors will become more important to the economies of Central Asian countries. Will Russia's fading economic position in Central Asia be viewed as sufficiently problematic to bring either a change in its international behavior, or call forth the need to flex Russia's military muscle? The latter could involve a Russia-backed separatist movement among ethnic Russians in East Kazakhstan, where ethnic Russians accounted for 36% of the 2018 population.[44] An opportune time for the latter option might occur during the leadership transition in Astana following the death of its aged leader, Nursultan Nazarbayev (born in 1940). Such an aggressive posture, however, would complicate Russia's relations with all of its neighbors, and would generate strong pressure in the U.S. and Europe to react with far harsher economic measures than those imposed following Russia's annexation of Crimea.

A New Team Focuses on the Domestic Economic Growth Within International Norms

This represents the only course with a chance to make Russia a success story. It is also the course with the greatest danger of leading the country to an internal breakdown (chaos). The latter could come either if reforms fail or when they begin to succeed. As the scholar Hannah Arendt pointed out in her seminal 1963 book, *On Revolution*, revolutions occur when things begin to get better and the population, developing rising and unfulfillable expectations, seeks to overthrow their country's leadership.[45]

China

Historically, a strong Russia (and subsequently USSR) created problems for China. These ranged from the Russian land grabs in 1858 and 1860 of the territory that now encompasses the Russian Far East to Beijing's very real fears of a Soviet nuclear attack in the late 1960s.[46] Today, by contrast, Russia is weak and does not represent a military threat to China, so even if Russian reform efforts succeed it will be some years before the balance of power between Russia and China is changed enough to merit a major reappraisal of the policies of both countries.

However, should those reforms fail, the situation would be very different. A weak Russia (1991 through the Putin era) has been good for China. The end of border tensions, strategic cooperation, and access to technologies and raw materials during this period significantly enabled the contemporary rise of China as a military and economic power. A continuation of the *status quo* can well be seen to be in China's interests. But if failed reforms begin to destabilize Russia, what are China's options?

Chinese decisionmakers who favor no drastic change may wish to economically assist the Russian government in return for concessions on natural resources or trade. Others, however, may wish to take advantage of Moscow's decline and advocate policies inspired by China's final defeat of its longtime Mongol enemies – a defeat accomplished largely through economic warfare and the territorial division of the Mongols.[47] This could mean that over a period of years or decades, Beijing may try to reclaim territories ceded to Russia in 1858 and 1860.

From Moscow's standpoint, any major reforms will need a minimum of external distraction. This means maintaining Russia's current, positive relations with China – even at the cost of giving more political and economic concessions to China. Such concessions could come in the form of trade negotiations (e.g., selling more sensitive military technology) or requests for greater strategic cooperation, such as a more muscular Russian naval presence in war games conducted in the South China Sea.

U.S. policy might also depend on Washington's assessment of the future failure or success of Moscow's reforms. An enduring Russian foreign policy built on adherence to international norms dictates help and cooperation while one built simply to buy the time and gain the strength necessary to resume its predatory international policies does not.

Russia's European neighbors

Europe, along with the U.S., will certainly welcome the relaxation of tensions with Russia, as this is necessary for any serious Russian reforms to have a chance of success. Indeed, Western European nations may be so hungry for such a relaxation that they pressure the U.S. to normalize relations very early in Russia's yet to be fully defined reform process. This will be especially true if Russia comes into increased compliance with treaties and international norms. Some countries in Eastern Europe – notably the Baltic States, Poland, and Ukraine – will be more cautious, because they are the most threatened and still have fresh memories of Russian or Soviet aggression. With fewer economic ties to Russia and because of its role as the main military guarantor of NATO states, the U.S. will feel less strategic need to quickly normalize relations with Russia. But internal political concerns on the part of the U.S. government may nonetheless nudge Washington in the direction of an expedited reconciliation with Moscow.

Treaty compliance and other international norms

The sooner Moscow credibly come into compliance with the Treaties listed in Appendix II, the sooner the U.S. and other countries currently hostile to Russia will move to change their anti-Moscow policies. Promises of compliance from Moscow and/or continued denial of its treaty violations will not be able to buy Russia the international freedom of action required for needed reforms at home. The key question is, as indicated above, at what point on the road to Russia's promised return to treaty adherence can the normalization of relations begin, and how quickly should those relationships be normalized?

Russia's internal empire

Relaxed tensions with the West, along with successful economic reform, holds the promise of containing or ameliorating separatist tendencies throughout Russia – especially if sufficient new money begins to flow to non-donor regions and donor regions are able to send less money to Moscow. The success of any reformist government will also hinge on its ability to: 1) create conditions favorable for foreign investment and 2) steer that investment to critical regions (e.g., the Russian Far East). This could involve the settlement of Russia's longstanding dispute with Japan over the ownership of the Kurile Islands, which the Soviet Union conquered at the end of World War II. It is thought that such an agreement would lead to massive Japanese investment in Russia's Far East. Large investment in the Far East could also come from China, though the resulting economic benefits may be judged less important than concerns over growing Chinese influence in that region.

A reformist government could also strengthen its support by returning some Putin-usurped power to regional governments. This might include restoration of local elections for governor, or the ability to independently levy local taxes and keep the resulting revenue.

In turn, if the U.S. comes to believe that Russia can be successfully reformed in a way conducive to a beneficial long-term bilateral relationship, it could take concrete steps to help assure that outcome – ranging from the encouragement of foreign investment in Russia to greater cooperation with Moscow on problems of mutual concern.

Russia and Central Asia

Russia's increased use of force in Georgia (2008), Ukraine (2014 to present) and Syria (2015 to present) has understandably caught the attention of the five Central Asian states, whose territories were brutally conquered by the Russian military in the 19th Century. For them, the success or failure of economic reforms in Moscow could significantly affect their own relations with a range of countries. In the wake of failed reforms, Russia might play a much smaller role in Central Asia. If so, which country (or combination of countries) would take Russia's place? China ranks highest on the list, which also includes majority Muslim countries in the Middle East, as well as the U.S. In this case, the U.S. may have to choose from two basic options: 1) to do nothing special to retard the influence of China and other countries in the so-called "post-Soviet space"; or 2) to encourage American investment at the same time implementing diplomatic efforts to support Central Asian countries in a way that ensures the influence of no single foreign power is dominant.

On the other hand, if reforms succeed, increased stability and economic power could lead to a more assertive Russian policy toward Central Asia – perhaps one whose strategic aim would be to "divide and dominate" the region. We could even see Moscow embrace a policy driven by the vision of Nobel laureate (and Russian nationalist) Alexandr Solzhenitsyn, and others, of a Greater Slavic State (Russia, Ukraine, Belarus, and North Kazakhstan).[48] Indeed this could become the rationale for Russia's territorial ambitions on its southern and western borders – something likely to bring stiff resistance from the West and perhaps from China as well.

Chaos

There are many scenarios for Russia descending into chaos. Perhaps the most comprehensive list of such possible futures is detailed in the Jamestown Foundation's 2016 book, *Eurasian Disunion*[49]:

> ...The prospects could include: violent power struggles between members of the ruling elite; the collapse of central authority; growing popular unrest because of falling living standards and shortages of products; regional turmoil generated by growing opposition to Moscow's policies; military mutinies, and the creation of private armies that splinter the country's defense structure; gang warfare between criminal organizations that increases chaos and ungovernability; the escalation of inter-ethnic disputes over power, territory and resources; the proliferation of ethnic, religious, regional and economic fiefdoms largely independent of the capital; an upsurge of violent Jihadism among radicalized Muslims in different parts of the Federation, especially in the North Caucasus and the Middle Volga; the growth of terrorism, sabotage, and the destruction of Russia's infrastructure; civil war in several parts of the country in escalating struggles for statehood, and the danger that weapons of mass destruction could fall into the hands of non-state militants.

The likelihood of any of the above is less pertinent than the general conclusion that Russia could become highly unstable if weakened centralized authority is not able to prevent the rupture of existing political fault lines. Therefore, let us examine the range of interlocking problems policy makers in both the U.S. and Russia could face under such circumstances.

China

Following China's 1685 defeat of Russian forces at Albazin, Beijing won much of the then-aboriginal territory that now encompasses much of the Russian Far East and part of Eastern Siberia. Chinese sovereignty over this area was formally recognized by the Russian-Chinese 1689 Treaty of Nerchinsk. However, by the 1850s, China became too weak to defend these territories and Russia conquered them. Russia's new sovereignty was formally recognized by treaties in 1858 and 1860.

Notwithstanding a July 2001 Sino-Russian treaty settling outstanding border disputes between them, a map illustrating "The Chinese Territories Invaded and Occupied by Tsarist Russia" continued to hang in Beijing's Military Museum for several years after. Indeed, as the author observed during several trips along both sides of the Russian/Chinese border in the 2000s, there is a feeling that, at some point, China will move to regain its lost territories.

But, even if the issue of sovereignty is put aside, China has two major economic needs that are unfulfilled.

WATER For many decades now, China has lacked an adequate amount of fresh water. In recent years, the shortage has become especially acute. Thus, in 2015, Wang Shucheng, China's former minister of water resources, warned that by the year 2020 "many northern cities, including the capital might run out of water."[50] Many Chinese feel the solution lies in the purchase of Russian water. But, primarily for ecological reasons, Russia has never agreed to sell its water to China.

Still, China and at least some Russian officials continue to pursue this dream. Two recent plans merit attention.
- In 2016, Russia's Agriculture Minister, Alexander Tkachev, proposed sending 70 million cubic meters of water from Russia's Altai region (destined to feed the Ob River) to China and eventually raising that total to one billion cubic meters.[51]
- Thereafter, 2017 saw Chinese planners announce a proposal to build a 620 mile pipeline to pump water from Russia's Lake Baikal to China's Gansu province.[52]

ARABLE LAND   During the author's 2001 trip to the Amur Valley, he was told by Vladimir Semenov, then Chairman of the Amur Oblast Duma, that Soviet-era studies projected that the rich black earth areas of the Amur Valley could accommodate a population of as many as 50 million people.

Today's total is a far cry from that. Russia's 2010 census showed 830,000 living in the Amur Oblast.[53] By way of comparison, the square mileage of the Oblast (140,000 square miles) is slightly bigger than the combined areas of Iowa, Indiana, and Ohio, but the population of those states is more than 25 times that of the Amur Oblast.

This vastly underpopulated region looks very appealing to millions of Chinese who would love to farm Amur's very rich soil, either as owners or renters. And while some Chinese are permitted to rent, efforts to import large numbers of Chinese farmers have yet to succeed. Most recently, in 2018, the government of Zabailkalsky Krai signed a preliminary agreement to give a Chinese company a 49-year lease on 1,000 square kilometers of land. This deal is now facing heavy opposition from Amur and other regions bordering China, which are scared that this represents a step toward their incorporation into the PRC.[54]

At the present time, there is little chance that China can reclaim its former, now Russian controlled lands or gain optimal access to Siberia's ample water supply and farm land. However, should an extended period of chaos come to Russia, Beijing might seek to change the *status quo*. Below are some ways this could happen, as well as a brief discussion of the policy options available to Washington as a result.

The four subdivisions of the Russian Federation that border China – Zabailkal, Jewish Autonomous Region (Yevrey), Khabarovsk Krai, and Primorski Krai – have a combined population that is under five million people and declining, while over 109 million people live in the Chinese provinces on the other side of the border (Heilongjiang, Jilin, and Liaoning).[55] This is a critical demographic problem for Russia. Currently, the Russian government is able to control the number of Chinese nationals on Russian territory. However, if chaos comes to Russia, the number of Chinese living in the Russian Far East will surely increase, as would Chinese influence. Russia could probably accommodate a million more Chinese in the Far East, albeit uneasily. But if five million Chinese moved into this area, thereby creating parity between the number of ethnic Chinese and Russians there, Russian sovereignty over the Far East would be far less secure. An ethnic Chinese population of 10 million would raise the possibility of the territory being annexed by China. Even if power in Moscow was later consolidated, the removal of Chinese citizens from Russian soil might not be possible. To do so would risk Chinese military intervention to protect ethnic Chinese.

Such use of China's very large population is not new to Beijing. It was through similar actions that the once-Russian city of Harbin became a Chinese city that today has very few permanent Russian inhabitants. China's restive western province of Xinjiang has seen its Han population rise from a post-World War II figure of under 10% to an estimated 50% in 2018.[56]

Under such circumstances, the U.S. might provide economic or diplomatic support to help Russia maintain control over this territory. Or alternatively, Washington might simply let local events take their own course.

In any case, large-scale Chinese migration to Russian territory would present local leaders in Russia's Far East (especially the northern parts, which are not as interesting to the Chinese) with some choices. They might explore the possibility of a resource-rich independent state guaranteed by Japan and/or Korea. The 30,000 residents of the remote Russia territory of Chuhotka, meanwhile, may pursue a different course. Because they are ethnically and linguistically related to the native peoples in neighboring Alaska, it is not inconceivable that these Russians might pursue closer and independent ties with the U.S.

Russia's European neighbors

During times of chaos, the reasons for Russia's past bad behavior, as well as the long-term intentions of Russia's new leadership, will matter far less to the Kremlin than Moscow's need to eliminate tensions with its European neighbors. Russian decision makers will likely have the same attitude toward the United States.

Treaty compliance and other international norms

As Appendix II demonstrates, Russia has regularly violated a host of treaties and agreements. This has been especially true during the most recent years of the Putin administration (which have seen infractions of the UN Charter, the Helsinki Treaty, the Budapest Accord, the New Start Agreement, and other relevant arrangements). While most new Russian governments would likely feel the need to lessen tensions with the West, a government that ruled during severe internal disorder would be under the most pressure to do so. A *sine quo non* for the West agreeing not to cause problems for the Russian government, and/or helping it politically and economically, should be Russian compliance with treaties previously signed.

Russia's internal empire

Russia is still an empire. A quarter of Russia's 2018 population of 144 million people is non-Russian, and the largest of those minorities dream of substantial autonomy or independence. Chief among them are the Chechen, Ingush, and Dagestani subdivisions of the North Caucasus (over 5 million souls in total), Tatarstan (3.8 million), and Bashkortostan (4.1 million). Further, even some rich Siberian regions with a majority ethnic Russian population have had similar thoughts.[57] Barring the complete collapse of centralized power, Moscow should be able to keep these restive regions as part of Russia. However, this is not a given. If the authority of Russia's central government lost its ability to govern remote regions, a regional Army commander aligned with the separatist leadership of a natural resource-rich area might declare an independent state (possibly with the support of a neighboring country). This would instantly make everyone on their team wealthy, as the new entity would divide profits from its oil, gas and mineral sales among themselves, as opposed to seeing that money go to Moscow.

In any case, Moscow may become so preoccupied that China sees an opportunity to renew its territorial ambitions. At the same time, the non-Russian republics of the former Soviet Union would likely gain time to strengthen their sovereignty as they faced a less aggressive Russian foreign policy.

Should such a process unfold, the United States would be faced with several options. It may chose to be a silent observer of this process. It could provide support for Moscow's efforts to control its regions, thus assuring a unified counterweight to a rising China. Or it could help the regions seeking to free themselves from Russia's heavy hand, much in the same way it assisted the now independent states that formerly were part of the USSR.

Russia and Central Asia

With the possible exception of China, Russia can least afford to lessen its diplomatic activity in Central Asia. Three major reasons drive this conclusion. 1) Should any former Central Asian state fall under the sway of Islamists, it would further destabilize Russia itself; 2) Central Asia is the path through which narcotics and other varieties of criminal activity enter

Russia; and 3) if Russia were to withdraw from Central Asia, the vacuum would likely be filled by China, further complicating regional relations with that country.

The U.S. also has strategic interests in Central Asia and would play a larger role should there be a lessening of Russian influence. On the other hand, we share Russia's strategic interest in having a secure secular leadership in the five former Soviet Central Asian states. The rise of Islamist forces in Central Asia is therefore neither in the interest of Russia nor the United States.

CONCLUSION

Be it for reasons of a natural death, voluntary retirement, assassination or a coup, Putin's reign will eventually end. In the aftermath of such a transition, any new Russian leadership will have to address Russia's longstanding internal political tensions. Their efforts will take one of three paths.

1. *Effective Repression.* Greater internal repression, accompanied by an aggressive foreign policy, could well buy time for a new Putin-like leadership. Greater internal repression, accompanied by a less aggressive foreign policy, might also provide additional breathing room. However, both courses would only postpone the day when Russia's worsening problems would have to be addressed. This confronts the United States with a key question: namely, can Russia's recent (and potentially future) violations of treaties and international norms be deterred, or alternatively be tolerated? For its part, Russia's new leadership may be forced to choose between risking its hold on power by moderating its foreign policies or pushing tensions with the West beyond the ability of either country to control.

2. *Serious Reform Efforts.* Major societal change is inherently dangerous because reforms need time to work and may make matters worse in the short run. Therefore, even if reform efforts in Russia are headed for success, there will be a window where opponents can effectively claim that those efforts are leading the country to disaster. The reform leadership may not be able to hold power under such circumstances, and are likely to look for help wherever it can be found. At that time, the United States (and the broader West) will have to engage in a "risk/reward" analysis based upon

the Russian regime's ability to survive (with or without Western aid) and to successfully implement promised reforms. This calculus is likely to become an ongoing exercise, as the Russian government zigzags between success and failure. If reform efforts ultimately succeed and Russia enjoys a sustained period of economic growth, the world will watch to see if Russia's newfound prosperity becomes the basis for more sustainable and aggressive actions against the West, or if the government drifts toward a greater embrace of international norms.

3. *Incompetent Execution of the First Two Options.* This would lead to internal disorder that would likely cause Moscow's leadership to avoid external problems as they focused upon the various threats at home. These threats could go well beyond the problems normally associated with the consolidation of power. In the worst case, they could include encroachment by China and/or internal terror and fighting leading to the *de facto* or *de jure* independence of the country's Muslim regions and parts of Siberia. Depending upon how events unfold, America may opt to be a bystander to these events, or actively involve itself on behalf of, or against, Russia's central government.

It is not possible to know when or how Russia's leadership will change. Nor is it possible to know what their policies will be or how competently these policies will be executed. However, at some point, and perhaps with little notice, the United States will have to decide how to engage a new Russian leadership. It is the author's hope that this monograph can provide an ongoing context by which government analysts can formulate appropriate responses to such possible changes.

ADDENDUM:
Succession Struggles in the USSR and Russia

I n all countries, individuals aspiring to power and their senior political teams study the successful and unsuccessful examples of those who came before them. In countries led by dictators, senior political operatives discuss the theory and practice of making a coup or organizing the type of "color revolutions" that previously toppled governments in Georgia and Ukraine. In democracies, they talk about the strengths and weaknesses of previous campaigns for President or Prime Minister. Of course, each country has its own unique circumstances, and Russia is no exception. Those wishing to replace Putin have and will continue to study how power has previously changed hands in Moscow, because employing at least some of those methods will be their path to success. Below are brief summaries of lessons learned when power changed hands in the USSR, and subsequently in post-Soviet Russia. The reader may find special interest in the part that describes the steps that Vladimir Putin took to consolidate his power.

How Joseph Stalin took and held power

When Vladimir Lenin died in January of 1924, Grigory Zinoviev (head of the Party in Leningrad and longtime head of the Comintern), and not Joseph Stalin (then General Secretary of the Party), was seen by many Soviets as Lenin's likely successor.[58] Additionally, Leon Trotsky (Founder and Commander of the Red Army), Lev Kamenev (Chairman of the Executive Committee of the Congress of Soviets), and *Pravda* editor Nikolai Bukharin also had substantial and independent bases of power. With the exception of then Politburo candidate Bukharin, all were members of the seven-person Politburo formed in 1917 to manage the revolution and the new country it created. (Bukharin became a full member of the Politburo upon Lenin's death in 1924.)

Prior to Lenin's death, and until his own, Stalin aggressively strove to place his own people in Party and/or government positions. Parallel to, and not incompatible with those efforts, were his moves to remove figures opposed to him from any position of power. By 1924, this power base was sufficient for Stalin to be part of the triumvirate (Stalin, Kamenev, and Zinoviev) that opposed Trotsky and jointly came to rule the USSR.

During the December 1925 Party Congress, Zinoviev launched a failed attack on Bukharin, whose principal backer was Stalin.[59] Following that Congress, Trotsky, Zinoviev, and Kamenev formed the United Opposition to oppose Bukharin and Stalin. They lost, and all three were expelled from the Politburo in October 1926. But it was another year before Stalin was able to also expel them from the Party in December 1927. In time, Zinoviev and Kamenev were executed following show trials, and Trotsky was assassinated in Mexico on orders from Stalin. All this, of course, was in line with the often repeated Stalin dictum, "no person, no problem."[60]

Still Stalin's power was not absolute. In April 1928, the Politburo condemned the excesses that had been committed by Stalin, and Bukharin called for Stalin's dismissal as General Secretary of the Party.[61] Stalin won narrowly, but his possession of uncontested power was still years away. In 1933, Bukharin was still strong enough to be permitted a speech at the Party Plenum. At that same forum, Stalin was forced to concede that he had made some mistakes.[62]

In the 1934 Party Congress, Bukharin spoke again and was re-elected to the Central Committee and given the editorship of *Izvestiya*. However, over the next few years Stalin obtained and kept total power through the killing and/or jailing of millions, including Zinoviev and Kamenev (executed in 1936) and Bukharin (executed in 1938).

Having eliminated both real and imagined domestic opposition, Stalin turned to foreign aggression. In September 1939, World War II began with the joint invasion of Poland by the USSR and its then-ally, Nazi Germany.

Joseph Stalin died in March 1953, at the age of 74. The death was probably from natural causes.

How Nikita Khrushchev took, held and then lost power

It is unclear exactly when Stalin died, but his death was officially announced on March 5, 1953. In the days before that announcement, the remaining leadership of the USSR began to cope with the reality that there was no clear line of succession. Who, or what group of people, would assume power?

Many Soviet experts felt that the logical choice was Georgy Malenkov.[63] Indeed, noted British Historian Hugh Seton-Watson went so far as to title his 1953 book *From Lenin to Malenkov: the History of World Communism*.[64] Seton-Watson, no doubt under a publisher's deadline, noted that in the aftermath of Stalin's death, Malenkov had assumed many of Stalin's titles.

Seton-Watson should have waited. Before the end of March 1953, Malenkov had resigned from his short-lived stint running the Party Secretariat, but remained on as Prime Minister. As a result, Khrushchev came to head the Party Secretariat and used it in the same way that Stalin did during his own rise to power, namely to control personnel assignments. However, the Secretariat was also useful as a source of political information – information regarding the desires and vulnerabilities of those whose support was needed by Khrushchev.

Following the military-assisted July 1953 purge of Lavrentiy Beria, Khrushchev became the junior member of the country's three-person collective leadership. Reminiscent of the 1920s Triumvirate, the Troika (named after a Russian carriage pulled by three horses) consisted of Georgy Malenkov, Nikolai Bulganin and Khrushchev.

By January 1955, after unsuccessful moves against a military-backed Khrushchev, Malenkov was removed as Prime Minister leaving Khrushchev the undisputed leader of the USSR. However, Malenkov remained on the Politburo and was part of the Politburo majority that almost ousted Khrushchev in 1957.[65] They failed because Khrushchev, with substantial help from Minister of Defense and World War II hero Marshal Zhukov, was able to rally the Communist Party's Central Committee (the larger group that elects the Politburo) to his defense. As result, Malenkov and other enemies of Khrushchev were expelled from the Politburo, the Central Committee and the Communist Party. In October 1957, Zhukov, who was seen as mounting a challenge to Khrushchev, was also removed from the Politburo and dismissed as Minister of Defense. No further serious challenges to Khrushchev's power were mounted until his fall from power in October 1964.

With domestic rivals under control, Khrushchev turned to foreign enemy number one: the United States. The installation of missiles in Cuba led to the Cuban missile crisis of 1962 and the real threat of war between the U.S. and the USSR – something that would become a major factor in Khrushchev's eventual fall from power.

How Leonid Brezhnev Seized and Held Power

General dissatisfaction with Khrushchev's rash and risky behavior during the Cuban Missile Crisis, his failed agriculture policy, and other matters gave the most ambitious of Khrushchev's fellow Politburo colleagues their opportunity. Quietly, Brezhnev, Nikolai Podgorny, and Alexander Shelepin began the dangerous game of approaching their colleagues until they succeeded in amassing the majority that ousted Khrushchev on October 14, 1964, and were able to deny him the right to involve the Central Committee in his defense. Remembering the role of the army in the events of 1957, care was taken to keep it on the sidelines. This was not too difficult a task, as the Army, by then, was dissatisfied with Khrushchev over a number of questions, including the military budget.[66]

In many ways, Brezhnev's consolidation of power looked very much like those of Stalin and Khrushchev before him. Following Khrushchev's removal, a new "troika" (Brezhnev, Podgorny, and Alexi Kosygin) took power and named Brezhnev First Secretary of the Communist Party, where he shared power with Podgorny (who was then Chairman of the Presidium of the Supreme Soviet).

Brezhnev became the Party's General Secretary in October 1966. Over the years that followed, he used this post to replace those who might not be loyal with loyalists or, at the minimum, individuals who would not rock the boat. He also moved against Anastas Mikoyan and Podgorny. Mikoyan was removed from the Chairmanship of the Supreme Soviet in December 1965, and taken off the Politburo in April 1966. By then, Brezhnev was seen as the dominant figure in Soviet politics. However, this did not mean he had absolute power. It took time to defeat Podgorny and others. In April 1966, Podgorny was removed as Second Secretary of the Central Committee and given Mikoyan's old (and largely ceremonial) position of Supreme Soviet Chairman. However, it was not until May 1977 that Brezhnev was strong enough to remove Podgorny from the Politburo, his real position of power. From the dismissal of Mikoyan until October 1980, Brezhnev also contended with the power of Aleksey Kosygin, who effectively ran the day-to-day activities of government. However, by the time the 76 year old Kosygin died in December 1980, he was no longer a serious rival to Brezhnev.

As was the case with both Stalin and Khrushchev, aggressive foreign military activities began once Brezhnev had consolidated power. In 1979, the USSR began its 10-year invasion of Afghanistan.

Leonid Brezhnev died of natural causes at age 75 in November 1982.

The rise of the short-term power holders

Two days after Brezhnev's death in November 1982, long-time (1967-82) KGB head Yuri Andropov defeated his Politburo rivals and was named General Secretary of the Communist Party. However, ill-health caused him to disappear from public view in August 1983, and he died in February 1984 at the age of 69.

In February 1984, after a three-month wait, the Politburo formally named Konstantin Chernenko as the Party's new General Secretary. As he was clearly in ill health at the time, he was viewed as simply a place holder. The then-73 year old Chernenko died thirteen months later, in March 1985.

How Mikhail Gorbachev took, held and then lost power

Gorbachev became a member of the USSR's Central Committee in 1971 and, under the patronage of the Politburo's second-ranking member, Mikhail Suslov, was named a candidate member of the Politburo in 1979 and a full member in 1980. Gorbachev, then the youngest member of the Politburo, was clearly being groomed for the country's top job. However, his ambitions suffered a setback when his mentor Suslov died some months before Brezhnev's death in 1982. Gorbachev, however, understood well the changed circumstances, and his vigorous activity during the short tenures of Andropov and Chernenko put him in a position to ascend to power the day after Chernenko's death in March 1985.

Like those before him, Gorbachev continued to consolidate his official powers, taking the reins of the Supreme Soviet in 1988 and assuming the newly created title "President of the USSR" in 1990. But his actual grasp on power was not as strong as it seemed to most observers. The presence of Gorbachev's rivals, both inside and outside the Politburo, was known in Moscow and, to varying degrees, in Western capitals. In Washington, DC, at a small American Foreign Policy Council-organized dinner in April 1990, *Pravda* editor and soon to be Politburo Member Ivan Frolov was addressed with the following dilemma: "The problems facing the Soviet Union today are too big to be solved by anyone. This is likely to bring a challenge to Gorbachev's rule. If that time comes, will he do what is necessary to keep power?"

Frolov's long and highly articulate response was both discreet and prescient. Yes, he noted, a challenge could come, but if defeating it meant spilling blood, Gorbachev would be unlikely to do so, as the man was determined to rule by peaceful means. However, that did not mean that a coup would succeed, as those mounting the challenge might not be competent enough to perservere.

The challenge to Gorbachev, when it came, did so from two directions. The first was from the team united behind Boris Yeltsin, the former Party boss in Sverdlovsk. Gorbachev had elevated Yeltsin, his then-ally, to the Politburo in 1986, but removed him in 1988 because of the latter's aggressive criticism of Gorbachev for the slow pace of reforms. However, by June 1991, Yeltsin had been elected President of the Russian Federation (then still a constituent part of the USSR) and was seen as the leader of those seeking democracy, a delegation of power to the regions, and movement toward a market economy.

The second and more immediate challenge to Gorbachev (as well as to Yeltsin) came from hardline anti-reform elements of the Soviet government and military. They stood for the centralization of power (order) and a substantial return to Soviet ways of governance. Their vision of, and the need for, "order" was explained by KGB Chairman Vladimir Kryuchkov in December 1990 in a speech on Russian TV.[67] Shortly thereafter, the KGB developed a plan (involving 300,000 arrest forms and 250,000 handcuffs) that could be taken in case a "state of emergency" was declared.[68] Kryuchkov and his allies (including Defense Minister Dmitry Yazov, Internal Affairs Minister Boris Pugo, and Premier Valentin Pavlov) pushed Gorbachev to declare a state of emergency. When he repeatedly refused to do so, they had forces surround his vacation home in Crimea on August 18, 1991 and allegedly told Gorbachev to sign the decree or resign. The next day, the hardliners (the so-called "Gang of Eight") ordered tanks onto the streets of Moscow and proclaimed themselves in control. As described in the following section, the coup failed. But by December 25, 1991, Gorbachev had lost all power and the Soviet Union ceased to exist.

Post-Soviet Leaders and How They Came to Power

How Yeltsin took and held power

Yeltsin's association with Gorbachev dated from the late 1970s, when Yeltsin was the Party Secretary of Sverdlovsk Oblast and Gorbachev was the party Secretary of Stavropol Krai. The relationship was good enough that Gorbachev brought Yeltsin to Moscow (and therefore to national politics) to tame the always important Moscow city government.

But, as noted above, Yeltsin made a series of risky moves to oppose

Gorbachev, his pace of reform, the Communist Party, and the continued centralization of power in Moscow. Having positioned himself as the acknowledged head of the movement representing these values, he was elected President of Russia (then one of 15 "republics" constituting the USSR) in June 1991. And when the August 1991 coup attempt began, Yeltsin used the political operation he had built to rally the regional elites on his behalf. Because the KGB monitored phone traffic, after a very tense initial 48-hour period it became increasingly clear to major Moscow institutions that Yeltsin, and not the coup plotters, had the support of the country. This support contributed to the army's decision to stand down with some units openly backing Yeltsin. Yeltsin had won. In the months that followed, Gorbachev, liberated from his captivity by pro-Yeltsin forces, returned to Moscow to be a bit player in the Yeltsin-led dissolution of the Soviet Union. By December 1991, Gorbachev was no longer a decisive factor in Russian politics.

But serious opposition to Yeltsin remained. Throughout 1992, a struggle for power took place between Russia's Parliament (the Supreme Soviet) and Yeltsin. A December 1992 compromise agreed to between Supreme Soviet Speaker Ruslan Khasbulatov and Yeltsin quickly fell apart. On March 28, 1993, the Supreme Soviet came within 72 votes of the 2/3 majority needed to impeach Yeltsin. Yeltsin called for a referendum (which he won on April 25th) on his rule and the need to hold early elections for the Duma and President. This result was rejected by the Supreme Soviet and, by May 1993, Supreme Soviet-inspired anti-government protests became violent.

By August 13, 1993, relations between the Supreme Soviet and the President had deteriorated to the point where an *Izvestiya* commentator declared: "The President issues decrees as if there were no (Parliament) and the (Parliament) issues decrees as if there were no President."[69]

What came next was best described by Yeltsin's then-Chief of Staff, Sergei Filatov, in his October 2003 interview with *Radio Free Europe/ Radio Liberty*:

> ...all contact was lost between the president and the parliament... We all had that Soviet, imperial mentality, where strength will always better solve the problem as opposed to negotiations and compromise... It wasn't an accident that we always supported the forceful option in solving this or that issue, which means that we didn't grow up to the level of ability to solve issues by peaceful means.[70]

On September 28th, blood was spilled in confrontations between police and anti-Yeltsin demonstrators. At the same time, Yeltsin's Interior Ministry forces sealed off the parliament building that then had an estimated 600 well-armed fighters of its own[71] – a number that would increase after the pro-parliament forces broke through the line established by Interior Ministry forces.

Things came to a head on October 3rd, when Yelstin's ambitious Vice President, Alexander Rutskoy, by then inside the parliament building, urged supporters to seize the office of Moscow's mayor (which was successfully done) as well as the national TV Center (which was stopped after fighting by Interior Ministry forces). At that point, elements of the army (which Yeltsin had ordered to intervene) decided to take Yeltsin's side. The Parliament building was shelled, killing some and wounding others. Understanding that they had lost, the Parliament leaders surrendered and were arrested. They would be released by Yeltsin in 1994 and charges against them were dropped the following year, when they were no longer capable of challenging Yeltsin's power. Estimates of the dead in the incident ranged from the official figure of 187 to over 2,000.[72] Yeltsin also used the aftermath of his victory over Parliament to ban leftist and nationalist organizations and papers.[73]

Yet Yeltsin's hold on power was still not fully secure. A December 1993 election for the new parliament (then called the Duma) was held, bringing to power a new group of people. However one counted it, Yeltsin's supporters were a minority of the new parliament which strongly opposed his economic policies.

But Yeltsin kept a base of support in the country. In the first round of Presidential elections in June 1996, he led the field of 11 candidates with 35.8% of the vote, outpacing the second place finisher, Communist Party leader Gennady Zyuganov, who commanded 32.5%.[74] In the July 1996 runoff, Yeltsin defeated Zyuganov 54.4% to 40.7%.[75]

Yeltsin's reelection victory came with the realization that he was in failing health. He suffered a heart attack between the first and second rounds of the election and was advised that he needed a multiple-bypass operation. That seven-hour surgery was successfully completed in November 1996. All this left Yeltsin looking for a way to step down that ensured he would not be arrested and that his family's by-then substantial wealth would not be confiscated.

His answer was found in the Russian constitution, which provided for the Prime Minister to take over the duties of the President should the office become vacant. Viktor Chernomyrdin, who began exercising the duties of a Prime Minister in December 1992 before assuming the formal title under the new constitution in August 1996, was not seen as a viable option, and was dismissed in March 1998.

Chernomyrdin's tenure was followed by that of three very short term Prime Ministers. Sergey Kiriyenko served for four months, Yefgenny Primakov for eight, and Sergei Stepashin for just three. Yeltsin viewed none of them as suitable successors.

Then came the appointment of Vladimir Putin (discussed in the following section) in August 1999. Yeltsin resigned the office of President on December 31, 1999 and, as described below, Vladimir Putin became the acting President.

How Putin took and held power

Following the failed August 1991 Putsch, Boris Yeltsin named Interior Minister Vadim Bakatin as the new head of the KGB – an institution with which he had frequently clashed. Bakatin's assigned mission was to "liquidate" the KGB.[76] Six months later, however, Bakatin was out and the KGB establishment was both victorious and once again on the rise.[77]

During the Soviet era, the Communist Party and military were checks on the KGB's power. However, after Yeltsin's rise to power and the dismantlement of the USSR, neither was strong enough to restrain any behavior by the SVR and FSB (Moscow's new names for the bulk of the old KGB organization).[78] The FSB, which had responsibilities inside of Russia's borders, began the process of enriching its own – a task made easier by the fact that all "businessmen" in Russia are guilty of something, and the FSB could send whomever they wished to jail.[79] Big bribes and property thefts became common. From this milieu rose St. Petersburg's Deputy Mayor, Vladimir Putin, who successfully weathered corruption scandals and advocated a very appealing vision of obtaining money and power for his core constituency (the SVR and FSB). These ideas earned him a substantial following within those institutions, as well as among oligarchs such as Boris Berezovsky who mistakenly thought Putin was controllable. With this backing Putin became head of the FSB in 1998. And when, for health reasons, Yeltsin chose to resign, the person who held the position of Prime Minister became important because the Prime Minister takes over if Russia's presidency is vacated. He, therefore, would have a leg up in the Presidential election constitutionally mandated to be held within three months of the Presidency becoming vacant.

In conversations with the author, former Russian Foreign Minister Andrei Kozyrev related that it was not initially clear whether Yeltsin would show his continued confidence in then-Prime Minister Sergei Stapashin or replace him with then-FSB chief Vladimir Putin.[80] When Putin was finally selected in 1999, he was chosen with the condition that Yeltsin and his family would not be prosecuted and that, for a period of time, he would keep part of Yeltsin's team, including the Kremlin's then-Chief of Administration, Alexander Voloshin. Putin was formally elected President of Russia in 2000, and kept his promises to Yeltsin. The Yeltsin family was not prosecuted and Voloshin stayed in his position until October of 2003. From that less-than-dominant start, however, Putin has masterfully consolidated power. He did so by strengthening his FSB base and, one by one, crushing all alternative centers of power. Some examples follow.

Strengthening the FSB base

Putin's first strengthened his FSB base and other parts of the former KGB. Even before being elected President, he sent a signal to all FSB and SVR officers by publicly laying flowers on the grave of former KGB head Yuri Andropov and restoring a bronze plaque in Andropov's honor to its original location on the façade of the old KGB and now FSB headquarters – a symbolic gesture signafying the primacy the secret police would possess in the post-Soviet system under his rule.[81]

More practical measures followed. Putin quickly signed into law a measure that gave all elements of the security services the right to intercept email traffic.[82] The practical effect of this was to help service members get rich by shaking down private business. And, as those various agents enriched themselves, their support for Putin grew.

Because holding official positions facilitated the accumulation of wealth and hence support of his presidency, Putin aggressively put his people in powerful positions. As early as May of 2000, 40% of office-holders appointed by Putin had a KGB background.[83] Over the years that followed, this percentage grew dramatically. Putin loyalists soon dominated the Defense and Interior ministries as well as the major state-owned companies.[84]

Nationalists and neo-imperialists were also courted. Putin was known to rue the collapse of the USSR, and in late 2001 he pushed the enactment of a law on the expansion of the territory of the Russian Federation[85] – a clear sign that he aspired to regain territory lost as a result of the collapse of the Soviet Union.

Centralizing power

Also in 2000, Putin sought to expand the powers of the Russian presidency. The KGB, split into several parts after the collapse of the USSR, was gradually put back together – primarily under the FSB and SVR structures. The power of independently elected governors was curtailed in 2000 when Russia's regions (then numbering 89) were grouped into 7 zones controlled by a Presidential envoy empowered to review all their records.[86] As virtually all Russians in public life had something to hide, this gave envoys the power to jail those governors and other local officials who did not go along with Putin's policies and/or provide payments to his cadre. Additionally, the envoys gained control of patronage in their respective regions – including the naming of local police force heads, thereby cementing their (and their bosses) hold on power.

Putin further consolidated his power via the Federal Law on Political Parties, which was amended several times during Putin's first decade in power.[87] This legislation provided the justification for limiting the number of legal political parties as well as using Putin-friendly courts and election officials to remove undesirable candidates for Duma elections.

By 2004, Putin was strong enough to end the direct election of governors and to double the size of Russia's bureaucracy. Of course, the new bureaucrats thereby given positions of power are presumed to be more loyal to Putin.

In the last few years, Putin has forbidden officials to own foreign assets through the use of a third party.[88] As this is a widespread practice, all who are vulnerable to prosecution for this practice have yet another reason to be loyal to Putin.

And in 2018, Putin established a political wing inside the Russian army as a way of having an early warning regarding any dissent with the military.[89]

Putting the oligarchs in their place

The oligarchs built their fortunes and exercised great influence under Russian President Boris Yeltsin. Those who helped Putin's rise to power (e.g., Boris Berezovsky) assumed that their influence would grow and even more money would be made. However, by 2003, Russia's richest oligarch, Mikhail Khodorkovsky, was in jail with much of his fortune divided among Putin's inner circle.[90] Others left or were forced out of Russia. In 2006, Russia asked Great Britain to extradite Berezovsky and Italy to expel Alexei Golubovich, thus proving that anti-Putin people were not safe even if they left Russia.[91] Most of the remaining oligarchs learned their lesson and made their own deals with the Kremlin – many standing ready to deliver anything the Kremlin desired.

Crushing the media

While Putin's efforts to solidify his base and centralize power were accomplished in a few years, Putin's nearly two decade-long effort to control the media is ongoing. It began in 2000 with a national security argument to justify the detention and harassment of journalists reporting on the Chechen War.[92] However, as time progressed, the national security justification was not needed and the targets became not just journalists but media properties themselves. Media owners, such as Vladimir Gusinsky, were given the choice of jail or a surrender of their media holding. Journalists were increasingly beaten, and sometimes killed.[93] Surviving newspapers were often forced to sign agreements with the pro-Kremlin Media Union and/or to put pro-Kremlin figures on their Board of Directors.[94] Outlets that would not cooperate had their broadcasting license terminated (e.g., *TV-6*) or their property seized (e.g., *Novaya Gazeta*).[95]

In 2002, FSB spokesman Gen. Alexander Zdanovich was put in charge of the body responsible for federal oversight of state-run radio and television. In 2003, he was given the right to shut down media outlets for "biased coverage."[96] Soon thereafter, Russia's sole remaining non-government national television station was taken off the air and replaced by a state-run sports channel.[97]

Subsequently, in 2004, Putin's government erected new, parallel structures to oversee the country's (already-compliant) media sphere, and to regulate the very pro-Putin Russian state television and radio. The first oversees management and the second, editorial policy.

With the national media tamed, efforts shifted to significant regional media outlets which were also brought under control. Current efforts to repress the electronic and print media focus on individual journalists who continue to be threatened with physical violence and sometimes murdered. Efforts to control the internet are described below.

Educating the young

Putin's effort to control the thoughts of his citizens also extends to education. As early as 2003, textbooks began to be reviewed for "political content," and books critical of the Kremlin that somehow managed to be published were seized.[98] By 2004 new textbooks began to appear with scarce mention of the gulags and "no place for pseudo-liberalism."[99] "Pseudo-liberalism" is also not found in the nationwide youth groups (akin to the Soviet-era Komsomol organizations) created to teach the virtues of Putinism.[100]

Cracking down on religious institutions and NGOs

Efforts to suppress alternative centers of thought residing in NGOs and religious institutions began in 2002, and have intensified over the last five years.

The first major efforts in this sphere occurred in 2002 with the enactment of a law permitting the activities of public and religious organizations to be suspended extra-judicially. Consistent with that law, restrictive actions were taken against all religions except Russian Orthodoxy, Buddhism, Islam, and Judaism.[101]

While Putin succeeded in placing his loyalists in the leadership of other Russian religious institutions (Islam, Judaism, etc.), Putin's relationship with the Russian Orthodox Church deserves special mention. Continuing the tradition of Czarist Russia and the USSR, the Orthodox Church's new Patriarch, Kirill, who has long been publicly known to have close ties to Russia's intelligence services, actively supports Putin while being allowed to enrich himself and those around him.[102]

With religious institutions suitably under his control, in 2012 Putin turned his attention to NGOs. During the following six years:

- Russia's upper house of Parliament released a "patriotic stop list" of twelve NGOs alleged to be a threat to national security.[103] The list includes three American organizations: the National Endowment for Democracy, (NED); the International Republican Institute (IRI) and Freedom House.
- Russia's only election monitoring organization, GOLOS, was forced to close after receiving very large government imposed fines.[104]
- The Kremlin began efforts to close down Memorial, a human rights organization founded by Nobel Laureate Andrei Sakharov, as well as other NGOs, including the Center for the Adoption and Training of Refugee Children.[105]

Repression of individual dissent

Between 2007 and 2017, Putin's efforts focused on the repression of individual dissent, including increased control of the internet. Putin's mastery of the electoral process became so complete that he could dictate the percentage of the vote he would receive. It became difficult, and dangerous, to hold peaceful protests unless the Kremlin found them useful. Organizing unsanctioned rallies became punishable with fines of up to $18,454[106]—an unmanageable sum for most Russians. Jury trials for those accused of "crimes against the state" were ended.[107]

Bloggers who logged more than 3,000 hits a day on their websites were required to register[108] with ROSKOMNADZOR, the country's official state censor, and their sites could be shut down without any justification or court order.[109] Internet "memes" were outlawed, and a new computer network was designed to scan social network sites and report anti-Putin activity.[110]

Most recently, in the tradition of the USSR, the Investigative Committee of the Russian Federation was created as a place for Russians to denounce their fellow citizens.[111]

How Does Putin Keep Power?

All of the above have helped Putin consolidate power. However, he still does not feel totally secure. Russia's President knows well the example of leaders who have been toppled by "color revolutions," as well as the fate of Romania's Nikolae Ceausescu and other dictators. As a result, Putin created his own private army in the guise of a National Guard (see page 16).[112] Further, Putin maintains his relationship with Chechen warlord Ramzan Kadyrov – thought to be Putin's private hit man whose own private army, the 30,000-strong Kadyrovtsy, provides Putin with further insurance against massive demonstrations that might be aimed at his overthrow.[113] Putin likewise stays close to others who have guns, namely the FSB (which is his political base) as well as the Army, which has a far greater capacity to use force. His need to stay close to the latter is likely a major reason why Putin has followed Boris Yeltsin's practice of taking vacations with Russia's Minister of Defense.

Repression can be effective, and likely this is enough to keep Putin from being toppled by large street demonstrations, unless they occur with the assistance and under the protection of a major part of the FSB and/or Army. However, repression does not provide absolute protection against the loss of support among the elite, who keep Putin in power.

Who are these elites, and why do they keep Putin in power? Russia is ruled by a Putin-led "party" that is comprised almost solely of those who have a history with the KGB and/or its successor organizations. They may work in government, become oligarchs, or work within the security services. The common thread is that they follow orders and support, or at least don't actively oppose, Putin. They do so for the following reasons.

Money

If one wishes to know what a society's elite believes about the future of their country, it is necessary to look no further than what they do with their money and their children. In Russia's case, most of the elite who collectively keep Putin in power send both abroad. They support Putin because: 1) he makes it possible for them to make or steal huge sums of money, and 2) he permits them to take substantial amounts of that money, and their children, abroad.

Nationalist/Imperialist/Great Power Ideology

Regardless of the increasingly obvious facts on the ground in Ukraine (e.g., widespread Ukrainian nationalism), many in Putin's inner circle agree with the sentiment articulated by former Russian Deputy Prime Minister Dmitry Rogozin in his 2003 book, *We Will Reclaim Russia for Ourselves*; namely, that "Russians... should discuss out loud the problem of a divided people that has an historic right to political unification of its own land... We must present ourselves with the problem of a union, no matter how unrealistic this idea is in today's conditions. And we must create conditions to result in the environment with which Germany dealt for forty years coming out united in the end."[114] These nationalists/imperialists support Putin's efforts to subvert Ukraine and eventually annex more of its territory. As long as Putin is seen as doing everything possible on this front, they will support him, including any implementation of a "two steps forward, one back" strategy. This strategic concept, advanced by Lenin, justifies tactical retreats (one step back) as long as they are followed by larger tactical advances (two steps forward).

The KGB Fraternity

Being a member of this "circle" demands loyalty of all who belong. Members of this fraternity make more money, have an easier time taking it abroad, and are excused sins that are not tolerated if committed by those outside this circle. In exchange for these benefits, loyalty is given to the top. Only a split within the top leadership of the FSB and SVR could cause members to oppose Putin.

Fear

Stories, long circulated in Moscow and perhaps apocryphal, have Putin criticizing Stalin because, "it was not necessary to kill so many to scare the others. Very visible killings or jailings of prominent people are sufficient to spread the necessary fear and to make sure that even those at a high level know they are not safe." In keeping with this idea, Putin has made examples of several high profile personalities:

In October 2003, Mikhail Khodorkovsky, then Russia's richest man, was arrested and began serving what would end up being 10 years in jail. The large majority of his assets were subsequently stolen by Putin's inner circle.[115]

In 2006, on the date of Putin's birthday (October 7th), well-known anti-Putin journalist Anna Politkovskaya, who hailed from an elite Moscow family, was assassinated in the elevator of her apartment building in a contract killing strongly suspected of being sanctioned by Putin.[116]

On February 27, 2015, Russia's former First Deputy Prime Minister and opposition activist Boris Nemtsov, was assassinated just steps from the heavily patrolled Kremlin in a not-so-subtle signal to regime opponents of the high costs of opposing the Kremlin.[117]

The list of such "cautionary tales" is long, and includes far more instances than those documented above. The common thread is that each victim was threatened with severe consequences if they did not stop their anti-Kremlin activities. They did not, and paid the price. The lesson is: "get in line or else." As a practical matter, not many want to be put on the list for retribution, whether such retribution would take the form of a confiscation of assets or death. This has led to passivity even among those who are highly critical of Putin.

ENDNOTES

1. Peter Frank, "The Changing Composition of the Communist Party," in Archie Brown and Michael Kaser, *The Soviet Union since the Fall of Khrushchev* (London: Palgrave Macmillan, 1978).

2. The World Bank, "Russian life expectancy at birth, male (years)," n.d., https://data.worldbank.org/indicator/SP.DYN.LE00.MA.IN?locations=RU.

3. Evgueni Andreev, Martin Mcee and Vladimir Shkolnikov, "Health expectancy in the Russian Federation: a new perspective on the health divide in Europe," *Bulletin of the World Health Organization*, 2003, http://www.who.int/bulletin/volumes/81/11/en/Andreevarabic1103.pdf.

4. U.S. Department of Health and Human Services, "Health, United States, 2016," May 2017, 114, https://www.cdc.gov/nchs/data/hus/hus16.pdf#014.

5. Ilan Berman, "Russia's Risky Syria Strategy," *The Journal of International Security Affairs*, Winter 2016, http://www.ilanberman.com/18585/russia-risky-syria-strategy.

6. "2018 Russia Military Strength", Global Fire Power, n.d., https://www.globalfirepower.com/country-military-strength-detail.asp?country_id=russia.

7. Frank Gibney, "Nikita Sergeyevich Khrushchev", *Encyclopaedia Britannica*, July 20, 1998, https://www.britannica.com/biography/Nikita-Sergeyevich-Khrushchev.

8. Andrew Osborn, "In Soviet Echo," Putin gives Russian army a political wing," Reuters, July 31, 2018, https://www.reuters.com/article/us-russia-military-politics/in-soviet-echo-putin-gives-russian-army-a-political-wing-idUSKBN1KL1VA.

9. Stanislav Lunev, "Changes may be on the way for the Russian security services," *PRISM 3*, no. 14, September 12, 1997, https://jamestown.org/program/changes-may-be-on-the-way-for-the-russian-security-services/.

10. "FACTBOX: Five facts about Russian military intelligence", Reuters, April 24, 2009, https://www.reuters.com/article/us-russia-medvedev-intelligence-gru-sb/factbox-five-facts-about-russian-military-intelligence-idUSTRE53N3K820090424.

11. "Profile: Russia's SVR intelligence agency", BBC, June 29, 2010, https://www.bbc.com/news/10447308.

12. "Putin Signs Law on Russian National Guard Troops," *Sputnik News*, July 3, 2016, https://sputniknews.com/russia/201607031042374664-putin-national-guard/.

13. "Russian National Guard Reaches 340,000 Men," *The Moscow Times*, November 25, 2016, https://themoscowtimes.com/news/russian-national-guard-reaches-340000-personnel-56308.

14. Charlie Gao, "This Is the Russian Special Forces Unit No One Talks about – Until Now," *The National Interest*, March 24, 2018, https://nationalinterest.org/blog/the-buzz/the-russian-special-forces-unit-no-one-talks-about%E2%80%94until-now-25055.

15. "7th Annual Warrior Competition Event, 2015," warriorcompetition.com, n.d., http://warriorcompetition.com/Pages/viewpage.aspx?pageID=25&ID=54.

16. Pavel Luzin, "The Ominous Rise of Russian National Guard," *Intersection*, July 21, 2017, http://intersectionproject.eu/article/security/ominous-rise-russian-national-guard.

17. "Ряды ФСКН поредеют", *интерфакс*, July 17, 2012, http://www.interfax.ru/russia/256063.

18. Svoboda, "Statistics of Drug Addiction in Russia: Figures and Facts," n.d., https://stop-zavisimost.ru/blog/statistika-narkomanii-v-rossii.html.

19. Steven Eke, "Russia: new rules hit foreign workers", BBC, n.d., http://www.bbc.co.uk/worldservice/specials/119_wag_climate/page9.shtml.

20. John Pike, "Federal Protective Service (FSO Federal'naya Sluzhba Okhrani", Federation of American Scientists, November 26, 1997, https://fas.org/irp/world/russia/fso/index.html.

21. "Text of Statute on Federal Security Service of Russian Federation and Structure of Federal Security Service Agencies", Federation of American Scientists, August 15, 2003, https://fas.org/irp/world/russia/fsb/statute.html.

22. Andrei Soldatov, "Putin Has Finally Reincarnated the KGB," *Foreign Policy*, September 21, 2016, https://foreignpolicy.com/2016/09/21/putin-has-finally-reincarnated-the-kgb-mgb-fsb-russia/.

23. See, for example, Olga Kuvshinova, "Number of 'donor regions' nearly halved over 10 years," *BMB Russia*, April 11, 2017, https://bearmarketbrief.com/2017/04/11/in-translation-number-of-russian-donor-regions-nearly--halved-over-10-years/.
24. Communist Party of the Russian Federation, "About Us," n.d., http://cprf.ru/about-us/.
25. Dmitry Kiselyov, "State TV Still Biggest and Most Trusted News Source for Russians – Poll," *The Moscow Times*, April 18, 2018, https://themoscowtimes.com/news/state-tv-still-biggest-most-trusted-news-source-russians-poll-61205.
26. Levada Center, "POLL: Informational Sources," April 18, 2018, https://www.levada.ru/2018/04/18/informatsionnye-istochniki/?fromtg=1.
27. Index on Censorship, "Russia: How one Radio Station Became a Target of Pressure, Threats and Extreme Violence," January 9, 2018, https://www.indexoncensorship.org/2018/01/russia-how-one-radio-station-became-a-target-of-pressure-threats-and-extreme-violence/.
28. Freedom House, "Freedom on the Net 2017," 2017, https://freedomhouse.org/report/freedom-net/2017/russia.
29. Ibid.
30. Ryan Browne, "Russia Follows China in Tightening Internet Restrictions, Raising Fresh Censorship Concerns," *CNBC*, July 31, 2017, https://www.cnbc.com/2017/07/31/russia-follows-china-in-vpn-clampdown-raising-censorship-concerns.html.
31. "Russia Tells Facebook to Localize User Data or be Blocked," Reuters, September 26, 2017, https://www.reuters.com/article/us-russia-facebook/russia-tells-facebook-to-localize-user-data-or-be-blocked-idUSKCN1C11R5.
32. Freedom House, "Freedom on the Net 2015," 2015, https://freedomhouse.org/report/freedom-net/2015/russia.
33. AGORA International, "Internet Freedom 2017: Creeping Criminalisation," n.d., http://en.agora.legal/fs/a_de-lo2doc/16_file_AGORA_Internet_Freedom_2017_ENG.pdf.
34. "Russia profile – Media," *BBC News*, April 25, 2017, https://www.bbc.com/news/world-europe-17840134.
35. See, for example, Elena Vartanova, "Russia – Media

Landscape," European Journalism Centre, 2018, https://me-dialandscapes.org/country/pdf/russia.

36. Committee to Protect Journalists, "Russia/Europe and Central Asia," n.d., https://cpj.org/europe/russia/.

37. House of Commons Foreign Affairs Committee, "Moscow's Gold: Russian Corruption in the UK," May 15, 2018, 6, https://publications.parliament.uk/pa/cm201719/cmselect/cmfaff/932/932.pdf.

38. Igor Bosilkovski, "Treasury Department's Russia Oligarchs List is Copied From Forbes," *Forbes*, January 30, 2018, https://www.forbes.com/sites/igorbosilkovski/2018/01/30/treasury-departments-russias-oligarchs-list-is-copied-from-forbes/#1dcf06946825.

39. "The world relies on Russia to build its nuclear power plants," *The Economist*, August 2, 2018, https://www.economist.com/europe/2018/08/02/the-world-relies-on-russia-to-build-its-nuclear-power-plants.

40. Andrei Kolesnikov, "Project Inertia: The Outlook for Putin's Fourth Term" Carnegie Moscow Center, January 25, 2018, https://carnegie.ru/commentary/75339.

41. Sean Ross, "Will Putin Ever Leave Office?", Investopedia, November 24, 2015, https://www.investopedia.com/articles/investing/112415/will-putin-ever-leave-office.asp.

42. Olga Khvostunova, "Andrei Kozyrev: 'Democracy Needs to Be Fought for Every Day,'" Institute of Modern Russia, July 14, 2018, https://imrussia.org/en/opinions/2971-andrei-kozyrev-%E2%80%9Cdemocracy-needs-to-be-fought-for-every-day%E2%80%9D.

43. Ibid.

44. Republic of Kazakhstan, Bureau of Statistics, "Slavic Population of the Kazakh Provinces of East Kazakhstan and West Kazakhstan," n.d., http://stat.gov.kz/faces/publicationsPage/publicationsOper/homeNumbersPopulation/homeNumbersPopulation-Ar2018?_afrLoop=4492079039724368#%40%3F_afrLoop%3D4492079039724368%26_adf.ctrl-state%3Dje-7sufvtz_56.

45. See generally Hannah Arendt, *On Revolution* (Penguin Classics, 2006).

46. Harrison E. Salisbury, *War between Russia and China*

(Bantam Books, 1970), 9.

47. For a more detailed discussion, see Morris Rossabi, *A History of China* (John Wiley and Sons, 2014).

48. Alexandr Solzhenitsyn, *The Russian Question* (New York: Farrar, 1995), 89.

49. Janusz Bugajski and Margarita Assenova, *Eurasian Disunion: Russia's Vulnerable Flanks* (Washington, DC: The Jamestown Foundation, 2016), https://jamestown.org/wp-content/uploads/2016/06/Eurasian-Disunion2.pdf.

50. Tom Phillips, "'Parched' Chinese City Plans to Pump Water from Russian Lake via 1000km Pipeline," *Guardian* (London), March 7, 2017, https://www.theguardian.com/world/2017/mar/07/parched-chinese-city-plans-to-pump-water-from-russian-lake-via-1000km-pipeline.

51. "Ambitious Plan to Divert Siberian Water to China gets Showered in Criticism," *The Siberian Times*, May 5, 2016, https://siberiantimes.com/ecology/casestudy/news/n0677-ambitious-plan-to-divert-siberian-water-to-china-gets-showered-in-criticism/.

52. Phillips, "'Parched' Chinese City Plans to Pump Water from Russian Lake via 1000km Pipeline."

53. Russian Federation, Federal Service for Government Statistics, "5. ЧИСЛЕННОСТЬ НАСЕЛЕНИЯ РОССИИ, ФЕДЕРАЛЬНЫХ ОКРУГОВ, СУБЪЕКТОВ РОССИЙСКОЙ ФЕДЕРАЦИИ, РАЙОНОВ, ГОРОДСКИХ НАСЕЛЕННЫХ ПУНКТОВ, СЕЛЬСКИХ НАСЕЛЕННЫХ ПУНКТОВ – РАЙОННЫХ ЦЕНТРОВ И СЕЛЬСКИХ НАСЕЛЕННЫХ ПУНКТОВ С НАСЕЛЕНИЕМ 3 ТЫСЯЧИ ЧЕЛОВЕК И БОЛЕЕ," n.d., http://www.gks.ru/free_doc/new_site/perepis2010/croc/Documents/Vol1/pub-01-05.pdf.

54. "Outcry in Russia over China Land Lease," *Financial Times*, June 25, 2015, https://www.ft.com/content/700a9450-1b26-11e5-8201-cbdb03d71480.

55. Dragos Tîrnoveanu, "Russia, China and the Far East Question," *The Diplomat*, January 20 2016, https://thediplomat.com/2016/01/russia-china-and-the-far-east-question/.

56. See Anthony Howell and C. Cindy Fan, "Migration and Inequality in Xinjiang: A Survey of Han and Uyghur Migrants in Urumqi," *Eurasian Geography and Economics* 52,

no. 1 (2011): 119-139, https://geog.ucla.edu/sites/default/files/users/fan/403.pdf; See also Anthony Ross, "Behind the Xinjiang Violence," *The Diplomat*, March 9, 2012, https://thediplomat.com/2012/03/behind-the-xinjiang-violence/.

57. "Siberians Increasingly Consider Themselves Siberians – Not Russians, Want Independence From Russia," *The Speaker*, July 27, 2014, http://thespeaker.co/headlines/siberians-increasingly-consider-siberians-russians-want-independence-russia/.

58. W.A. Ryser, "Malenkov Considered Top Choice to Succeed Stalin," UPI, March 4, 1953, https://www.upi.com/Archives/1953/03/04/Malenkov-considered-top-choice-to-succeed-Stalin/7641141927209/.

59. Encyclopaedia Britannica, "Nikolay Bukharin," n.d., https://www.britannica.com/biography/Nikolay-Ivanovich-Bukharin.

60. Richard Pipes, "'Death Solves All Problems,' He Said," *New York Times*, November 10, 1991, https://www.nytimes.com/1991/11/10/books/death-solves-all-problems-he-said.html.

61. Stephen Cohen, "Why Bukharin's Ghost Still Haunts Moscow," *New York Times*, December 10, 1978, https://www.nytimes.com/1978/12/10/archives/why-bukharins-ghost-still-haunts-moscow.html.

62. John Getty and Oleg Naumov, *The Road to Terror: Stalin and the Self-Destruction of the Bolsheviks*, 1932-1939 (New Haven: Yale University Press, 2008), 95.

63. Ryser, "Malenkov Considered Top Choice to Succeed Stalin."

64. Hugh Seton-Watson, *From Lenin to Malenkov: The History of World Communism* (New York: Praeger, 1957)

65. "Georgy Maksimilianovich Malenkov," E*ncyclopaedia Britannica*, July 20, 1998, https://www.britannica.com/biography/Georgy-Maksimilianovich-Malenkov.

66. Alden Whitman, "Khruschev's Human Dimensions Brought Him to Power and to His Downfall," *New York Times*, September 12, 1971, http://movies2.nytimes.com/learning/general/onthisday/bday/0417.html.

67. J. Michael Waller, "KGB: The Perils of Arbitrary Power," *Perspective* 2, no. 1 (September 1991), https://open.bu.edu/

handle/2144/3471.

68. Christopher Andrew, *The Sword and the Shield: The Mitrokhin Archive and the Secret History of the KGB* (New York: Basic Books, 2000), 393.

69. John Carey and Matthew Shugart, *Executive Decree Authority* (Cambridge: Cambridge University Press, 1998), 76.

70. "Who Was Who? The Key Players in Russia's Dramatic October 1993 Showdown," *Radio Free Europe/Radio Liberty*, October 2, 2018, https://www.rferl.org/a/russia-players-1993-crisis/25125000.html.

71. Serge Schmemann, "Revolt in Moscow: How Yeltsin Turned the Tide, Hour by Hour," *New York Times*, October 11, 1993, https://www.nytimes.com/1993/10/11/world/revolt-in-moscow-how-yeltsin-turned-the-tide-hour-by-hour.html.

72. Esther Fein, "Yeltsin Bans Communist Groups in Government," *New York Times*, July 21, 1991, https://www.nytimes.com/1991/07/21/world/yeltsin-bans-communist-groups-in-government.html.

73. Ibid.

74. "Results of Presidential Elections, 1996-2004," *Russia Votes*, August 12, 2015, http://www.russiavotes.org/president/presidency_96-04.php.

75. Ibid.

76. Vincent Schodolski, "New Director to 'Liquidate' KGB," *Chicago Tribune*, August 30, 1991, https://www.chicagotribune.com/news/ct-xpm-1991-08-30-9103050207-story.html.

77. Stella Rimington, "The Spy Who Went into the Cold," *Guardian* (London), September 11, 2001, https://www.theguardian.com/politics/2001/sep/12/freedomofinformation.uk.

78. Andrei Soldatov and Irina Borogan, "Russia's New Nobility: The Rise of the Security Services in Putin's Kremlin," *Foreign Affairs* 89, no. 5 (September/October 2010), 80-96.

79. Celestine Bohlen, "Yeltsin Resigns, Naming Putin as Acting President to Run in March Election," *New York Times*, January 1, 2000, https://www.nytimes.com/2000/01/01/world/yeltsin-resigns-overview-yeltsin-resigns-naming-putin-acting-president-run-march.html.

80. James Lewis, "Reference Note on Russian Communications Surveillance," Center for Strategic & International Studies, April 18, 2014, https://www.csis.org/analysis/reference-note-russian-communications-surveillance.

81. Brian Whitmore, "Andropov's Ghost," *Radio Free Europe/Radio Liberty*, February 9, 2009, https://www.rferl.org/a/Andropovs_Ghost/1467159.html.

82. Lewis, "Reference Note on Russian Communications Surveillance."

83. Arnold Beichman. "Putin's Revealing Personnel Choices". *Washington Times*. February 7, 2000. http://www.russialist.org/archives/4096.html#10.

84. Peter Baker and Susan B. Glasser. "In Kremlin Shuffle, Putin Puts Loyalists in Key Security Positions," *Washington Post*, March 29, 2001, https://www.washingtonpost.com/archive/politics/2001/03/29/in-kremlin-shuffle-putin-puts-loyalists-in-key-security-jobs/99ce4a2b-a362-4b26-89d5-ad968310f222/?utm_term=.df9408f10a96.

85. World Trade Organization, "On the Plenipotentiary Representative of the President of the Russian Federation in the Federal Okrug," Decree of the President of the Russian Federation No. 849, May 13, 2000, https://www.wto.org/english/thewto_e/acc_e/rus_e/wtaccrus48a5_leg_38.pdf.

86. World Trade Organization. "On the Plenipotentiary Representative of the President of the Russian Federation in the Federal Okrug". Decree of the President of the Russian Federation No. 849. May 13, 2000. https://www.wto.org/english/thewto_e/acc_e/rus_e/wtaccrus48a5_leg_38.pdf.

87. Seth Mydans and Erin Arvedlund, "Police in Russia Seize Oil Tycoon," *New York Times*, October 26, 2003, https://www.nytimes.com/2003/10/26/world/police-in-russia-seize-oil-tycoon.html.

88. "Russia's Putin Tightens Grip on Elites with Overseas Asset Ban," Reuters, August 29, 2013, https://www.reuters.com/article/russia-assets/russias-putin-tightens-grip-on-elites-with-overseas-asset-ban-idUSL6N0GS3U420130829.

89. "Britain Refuses to Extradite Berezovsky," *Radio Free Europe/Radio Liberty*, June 6, 2006, https://www.rferl.org/a/1068936.html.

90. "Russia Sends Italy Extradition Request for ex-Yukos

Director," *Sputnik*, May 16, 2006, https://sputniknews.com/russia/2006051648221657/.

91. "Arrest of Journalist, Blanket Media Restrictions on Chechnya Condemned," Human Rights Watch, January 31, 2000, https://www.hrw.org/news/2000/01/31/arrest-journalist-blanket-media-restrictions-chechnya-condemned.

92. Roy Greenslade, "Journalistic Death Toll in Putin's Russia," *Guardian* (London), March 11, 2012, https://www.theguardian.com/media/greenslade/2012/mar/11/journalist-safety-vladimir-putin.

93. Alexey Kovalev, "In Putin's Russia, the Hollowed-Out Media Mirrors the State," *Guardian* (London), March 24, 2017, https://www.theguardian.com/commentisfree/2017/mar/24/putin-russia-media-state-government-control.

94. Ian Traynor, "Kremlin's Last TV Critic Silenced," *Guardian* (London), January 11, 2002, https://www.theguardian.com/world/2002/jan/12/russia.media.

95. Alexey Kovalev, "In Putin's Russia, the hollowed out media mirrors the state," *Guardian* (London), March 24, 2017, https://www.theguardian.com/commentisfree/2017/mar/24/putin-russia-media-state-government-control.

96. Nick Patton Walsh, "Putin Angry at History Book Slur," *Guardian* (London), January 14, 2004, https://www.theguardian.com/world/2004/jan/14/books.russia.

97. Sophie Lambroschini, "Russia: Is the Education Ministry trying to Rewrite History?" *Radio Free Europe/Radio Liberty*, January 30, 2004, https://www.rferl.org/a/1051381.html.

98. Steven Lee Meyers, "Youth Groups Created by Kremlin Serve Putin's Cause," *New York Times*, July 8, 2007, https://www.nytimes.com/2007/07/08/world/europe/08moscow.html.

99. Lambroschini, "Russia: Is the Education Ministry trying to Rewrite History?"

100. David Satter, "Putin Runs the Russian State – and the Russian Church Too," *Forbes*, February 20, 2009, https://www.forbes.com/2009/02/20/putin-solzhenitsyn-kirill-russia-opinions-contributors_orthodox_church.html#492d-9cf13bf9.

101. "Russia: Four Years of Putin's 'Foreign Agents' Law to Shackle and Silence NGOs," Amnesty International,

November 18, 2016, https://www.amnesty.org/en/latest/news/2016/11/russia-four-years-of-putins-foreign-agents-law-to-shackle-and-silence-ngos/.

102. Alissa de Carbonnel, "Russian Vote Watchdog among Thousands of NGOs Facing Fines, Closure," Reuters, April 9, 2013, https://www.reuters.com/article/us-russia-ngos-idUSBRE9380Q120130409.

103. "PRESS RELEASE: Human Rights: Closing Down of Russian Memorial NGO; Uzbekistan; Mexico," European Parliament, December 23, 2014, http://www.europarl.europa.eu/news/en/press-room/20141016IPR74265/human-rights-closing-down-of-russian-memorial-ngo-uzbekistan-mexico.

104. David Herszenhorn, "New Russian Law Assesses Heavy Fines on Protesters," *New York Times*, June 8, 2012, https://www.nytimes.com/2012/06/09/world/europe/putin-signs-law-with-harsh-fines-for-protesters-in-russia.html?mtrref=www.google.com&gwh=B2DFDF759B9B-1253F64E36FB4A2821D3&gwt=pay.

105. "Russia Enacts 'Draconian' Law for Bloggers and Online Media," BBC, August 1, 2014, https://www.bbc.com/news/technology-28583669.

106. Michael Birnbaum, "Russian Blogger Law puts New Restrictions on Internet Freedoms," *Washington Post*, July 31, 2014, https://www.washingtonpost.com/world/russian-blogger-law-puts-new-restrictions-on-internet-freedoms/2014/07/31/42a05924-a931-459f-acd2-6d08598c375b_story.html?utm_term=.8cb244216316.

107. Nick Holdsworth, "Russia scraps right to jury trial," *Telegraph* (London), December 12, 2008, https://www.telegraph.co.uk/news/worldnews/europe/russia/3725300/Russia-scraps-right-to-jury-trial.html.

108. Avi Selk and David Filipov, "It's now Illegal in Russia to Share an Image of Putin as a Gay Clown," *Washington Post*, April 5, 2017, https://www.washingtonpost.com/news/worldviews/wp/2017/04/05/its-now-illegal-in-russia-to-share-an-image-of-putin-as-a-gay-clown/?utm_term=.c97c4934f00f.

109. Kremlin, "Executive Order on Creation of Investigative Committee of the Russian Federation," September 27, 2010. Detailed at http://en.kremlin.ru/events/president/news/9037.

110. Marvin Kalb, "Why Putin Needs a Praetorian Guard," Brookings Institute, May 3, 2017, https://www.brookings.edu/blog/order-from-chaos/2017/05/03/why-putin-needs-a-praetorian-guard/.

111. Kremlin, "Executive Order on Creation of Investigative Committee of Russian Federation."

112. Kalb, "Why Putin Needs a Praetorian Guard."

113. Tom Balmforth, "Opposition Calls Kadyrov 'Private Army' Threat to Russia," *Radio Free Europe/Radio Liberty*, February 22, 2016, https://www.rferl.org/a/russia-chechnya-kadyrov-private-army-threat-opposition-report/27567375.html.

114. As cited in Herman Pirchner, Jr. *Reviving Greater Russia: The Future of Russia's Borders with Belarus, Georgia, Kazakhstan and Ukraine* (Lanham, MD: University Press of America, 2005), 3.

115. Anne Applebaum, "How He and His Cronies Stole Russia," *New York Review of Books*, December 18, 2014, https://www.nybooks.com/articles/2014/12/18/how-he-and-his-cronies-stole-russia/.

116. Shaun Walker, "The Murder that Killed Free Media in Russia," *Guardian* (London), October 5, 2016, https://www.theguardian.com/world/2016/oct/05/ten-years-putin-press-kremlin-grip-russia-media-tightens.

117. David Satter, "Who Killed Boris Nemtsov?" *National Review*, October 31, 2017, https://www.nationalreview.com/2017/10/boris-nemtsov-assassination-russia-evidence-vladimir-putin-regime-guilty-chechen-leader-ramzan-kadyrov/.

ABOUT THE AUTHOR

Herman Pirchner, Jr. has been President of the American Foreign Policy Council (AFPC), a foreign affairs and national security think tank headquartered in Washington, DC, since its founding in 1982. Previously, Mr. Pirchner served in senior staff positions in the U.S. Senate. A leading expert on Russia and the "post Soviet space," he is the author of many publications on Russian policy and ideology. His 2005 book *Reviving Greater Russia: The Future of Russia's Borders with Belarus, Georgia, Kazakhstan, Moldova and Ukraine* (University Press of America) presciently foreshadowed Russia's subsequent aggression against both Georgia and Ukraine.

APPENDICES

APPENDIX I (SORTED BY COUNTRY)

Country	Dictator	Exit from Power	Age at Exit	Period of Rule
Algeria	Houari Boumediene	Natural Causes	46*	1965-1978
Algeria	Chadli Bendjedid	Forced Retirement	63	1979-1992
Algeria	Abdelaziz Bouteflika	Still in Power	N/A	1999-present
Angola	Agostinho Neto	Natural Causes	57*	1975-1979
Angola	Jose Eduardo dos Santos	Voluntary Retirement	75	1979-2017
Argentina	Juan Carlos Onganía	Forced Retirement	56	1966-1970
Argentina	Pedro Eugenio Aramburu	Killed in Office	67 *	1955-1958
Argentina	Alejandro Agustin Lanusse	Forced Retirement	54	1971-1973
Argentina	Roberto Eduardo Viola	Forced Retirement	57	March 1981-December 1981
Argentina	Reynaldo Bignone	Voluntary Retirement	55	1982-1983
Argentina	Leopoldo Galtieri	Forced Retirement	56	1981-1982
Argentina	Jorge Rafael Videla	Voluntary Retirement	55	1976-1981
Bangladesh	Ziaur Rahman	Killed in Office	45 *	1977-1981

Brazil	Emilio Garrastazu Medici	Voluntary Retirement	73	1969-1974
Brazil	Artur da Costa e Silva	Natural Causes	69 *	1967-1969
Brazil	Getúlio Vargas	Forced Retirement	63	1930-1945
Brazil	Humberto de Alencar Castelo Branco	Voluntary Retirement	69	1964-1967
Burkina Faso	Thomas Sankara	Killed in Office	37 *	1983-1987
Burundi	Jean-Baptiste Bagaza	Forced Retirement	41	1976-1987
Cambodia	Hun Sen	Still in Power	N/A	1984-present
Cambodia	Pol Pot	Forced Retirement	56	1963-1981
Cameroon	Paul Biya	Still in Power	N/A	1982-present
Chad	Francois Tombalbaye	Killed in Office	56 *	1960-1975
Chad	Hissene Habre	Forced Retirement	48	1982-1990
Chad	Idriss Deby	Still in Power	N/A	1990-present
Chile	Augusto Pinochet	Forced Retirement	75	1973-1990
China	Xi Jinping	Still in Power	N/A	2012-present
China	Hu Jintao	Voluntary Retirement	70	2002-2012

Country	Leader	Exit	Age	Years
China	Deng Xiaoping	Voluntary Retirement	82	1982-1987
China	Mao Zedong	Natural Causes	82 *	1943-1976
China	Chiang Kai-shek	Natural Causes	87 *	1950-1975
Colombia	Gustavo Rojas Pinilla	Forced Retirement	57	1953-1957
Cote d'Ivoire	Felix Houphouet-Boigny	Natural Causes	88 *	1960-1993
Cuba	Fidel Castro	Voluntary Retirement	85	1961-2011
Cuba	Raul Castro	Voluntary Retirement	86	2011-2018
Cuba	Fulgencio Batista	Forced Retirement	58	1952-1959
Democratic Republic of Congo	Mobutu Sese Seko	Forced Retirement	66	1965-1997
Egypt	Abdel Fattah el-Sisi	Still in Power	N/A	2014-present
Egypt	Hosni Mubarak	Forced Retirement	83	1981-2011
Egypt	King Farouk	Forced Retirement	32	1936-1952
Egypt	Gamal Abdel Nasser	Natural Causes	52 *	1956-1970
Egypt	Anwar Sadat	Killed in Office	62 *	1970-1981
Ethiopia	Haile Selassie	Forced Retirement	82 *	1930-1974

Ethiopia	Mengistu Haile Mariam	Forced Retirement	54	1977-1991
Germany	Adolf Hitler	Killed in Office	56 *	1933-1945
Ghana	Jerry Rawlings	Voluntary Retirement	53	1981-2001
Greece	Georgios Papadopoulos	Forced Retirement	54	1967-1973
Greece	Ioannis Metaxas	Natural Causes	69 *	1936-1941
Guatemala	Carlos Castillo Armas	Killed in Office	43 *	1954-1957
Guinea	Moussa Dadis Camara	Forced Retirement	45	2008-2009
Guinea	Ahmed Sekou Toure	Natural Causes	62 *	1958-1984
Haiti	Francois Duvalier	Natural Causes	64 *	1957-1971
Haiti	Jean-Claude Duvalier	Forced Retirement	35	1971-1986
Indonesia	Muhammad Suharto	Forced Retirement	67	1968-1998
Iran	Ali Khamenei	Still in Power	N/A	1989-present
Iran	Ruhollah Khomeini	Natural Causes	86 *	1979-1989
Iraq	Saddam Hussein	Forced Retirement	63	1979-2003
Iraq	Abd Al-Karim Qasim	Killed in Office	49 *	1958-1963
Italy	Benito Mussolini	Forced Retirement	60	1922-1943

Kazakhstan	Nursultan Nazarbayev	Still in Power	N/A	1991-present
Kenya	Daniel arap Moi	Voluntary Retirement	78	1978-2002
Malawi	Hastings Kamuzu Banda	Forced Retirement	95	1966-1994
Mali	Modibo Keita	Forced Retirement	53	1960-1968
Mali	Moussa Traore	Forced Retirement	54	1968-1991
Myanmar	Ne Win	Forced Retirement	78	1962-1988
Myanmar	Than Shwe	Voluntary Retirement	77	1992-2011
Nigeria	Sani Abacha	Killed in Office	54 *	1993-1998
Nigeria	Johnson Aguiyi-Ironsi	Killed in Office	42 *	Jan 1966-July 1966
Nigeria	Yakubu Gowon	Forced Retirement	41	1966-1975
Nigeria	Ibrahim Babangida	Forced Retirement	52	1985-1993
Nigeria	Olusegun Obasanjo	Voluntary Retirement	70	1976-1979
North Korea	Kim Il-Sung	Natural Causes	82 *	1948-1994
North Korea	Kim Jong-Il	Natural Causes	70 *	1994-2011
North Korea	Kim Jong-Un	Still in Power	N/A	2011-present
Pakistan	Pervez Musharraf	Forced Retirement	65	2001-2008

Pakistan	Agha Muhammad Yahya Khan	Forced Retirement	54	1969-1971
Pakistan	Ayub Khan	Forced Retirement	61	1958-1969
Peru	Alberto Fujimori	Forced Retirement	62	1990-2000
Peru	Manuel Odria	Voluntary Retirement	60	1948-1956
Philippines	Rodrigo Duterte	Still in Power	N/A	2016-present
Philippines	Ferdinand Marcos	Forced Retirement	69	1965-1986
Poland	Wojciech Jaruzelski	Voluntary Retirement	67	1981-1990
Portugal	Antonio de Oliveira Salazar	Natural Causes	79 *	1932-1968
Portugal	Marcelo Caetano	Forced Retirement	68	1968-1974
Romania	Ion Antonescu	Forced Retirement	62	1940-1944
Romania	King Michael	Forced Retirement	25	1940-1947
Romania	Nicolae Ceausescu	Killed in Office	71 *	1965-1989
Russia	Josef Stalin	Natural Causes	74 *	1924-1953
Russia	Nikita Khrushchev	Forced Retirement	70	1953-1964
Russia	Leonid Brezhnev	Natural Causes	75 *	1964-1982
Russia	Vladimir Putin	Still in Power	N/A	2000-present

Rwanda	Juvenal Habyarimana	Killed in Office	57 *	1973-1994
Rwanda	Paul Kagame	Still in Power	N/A	2000-present
Rwanda	Jean Kambanda	Forced Retirement	39 *	1994-1994
Saudi Arabia	Abdullah bin Abdulaziz Al Saud	Natural Causes	90 *	2005-2015
Somalia	Mohamed Siad Barre	Forced Retirement	71	1969-1991
South Korea	Syngman Rhee	Forced Retirement	85	1948-1960
South Korea	Park Chung-hee	Killed in Office	61 *	1963-1979
Spain	Francisco Franco	Natural Causes	82	1936-1975
Sudan	Omar al-Bashir	Still in Power	N/A	1989-present
Sudan	Gaafar Nimeiry	Forced Retirement	55	1969-1985
Syria	Hafez al-Assad	Natural Causes	69 *	1971-2000
Syria	Bashar al-Assad	Still in Power	N/A	2000-present
Thailand	Prayut Chan-o-cha	Still in Power	N/A	2014-present
Thailand	Plaek Phibun-songkhram	Forced Retirement	60	1938-1944, 1948-1957

Thailand	Thanom Kittikachorn	Forced Retirement	62	1963-1973
Thailand	Thaksin Shinawatra	Forced Retirement	57	2001-2006
Thailand	Sarit Thanarat	Natural Causes	55 *	1959-1963
Thailand	Kriangsak Chamanan	Voluntary Retirement	62	1977-1980
Thailand	Chatichai Choonhavan	Forced Retirement	70	1988-1991
Thailand	Surayud Chulanot	Voluntary Retirement	64	2006-2008
Tunisia	Zine El Abidine Ben Ali	Forced Retirement	74	1987-2011
Turkey	Recep Tayyip Erdogan	Still in Power	N/A	2014-present
Uganda	Idi Amin	Forced Retirement	53	1971-1979
Uganda	Milton Obote	Forced Retirement	46	1966-1971
Uganda	Milton Obote	Forced Retirement	60	1980-1985
Uzbekistan	Islam Karimov	Natural Causes	78 *	1991-2016
Uzbekistan	Shavkat Mirziyoyev	Still in Power	N/A	2016-present
Venezuela	Nicolas Maduro	Still in Power	N/A	2013-present
Venezuela	Hugo Chavez	Natural Causes	58 *	1999-2013
Venezuela	Marcos Pérez Jiménez	Forced Retirement	44	1948-1958

Vietnam	Ho Chi-Minh	Natural Causes	79 *	1951-1969
Yugoslavia (1989)	Tito	Natural Causes	87 *	1953-1980
Yugoslavia (1989)	Slobodan Milosevic	Forced Retirement	60	1989-2000
Zambia	Kenneth Kaunda	Voluntary Retirement	67	1964-1991
Zimbabwe	Robert Mugabe	Forced Retirement	93	1980-2017

Appendix I (Sorted by cause of death)

Mode of Exit from Power	Country	Dictator	Age at Exit	Period of Rule
Forced Retirement	Algeria	Chadli Bendjedid	63	1979-1992
Forced Retirement	Argentina	Juan Carlos Onganía	56	1966-1970
Forced Retirement	Chad	Hissene Habre	48	1982-1990
Forced Retirement	Chile	Augusto Pinochet	75	1973-1990
Forced Retirement	Colombia	Gustavo Rojas Pinilla	57	1953-1957
Forced Retirement	Cuba	Fulgencio Batista	58	1952-1959
Forced Retirement	Democratic Republic of Congo	Mobutu Sese Seko	66	1965-1997
Forced Retirement	Egypt	Hosni Mubarak	83	1981-2011
Forced Retirement	Egypt	King Farouk	32	1936-1952
Forced Retirement	Ethiopia	Haile Selassie	82 (Died in office)	1930-1974
Forced Retirement	Ethiopia	Mengistu Haile Mariam	54	1977-1991
Forced Retirement	Greece	Georgios Papadopoulos	54	1967-1973

Forced Retirement	Guinea	Moussa Dadis Camara	45	2008-2009
Forced Retirement	Haiti	Jean-Claude Duvalier	35	1971-1986
Forced Retirement	Indonesia	Muhammad Suharto	67	1968-1998
Forced Retirement	Iraq	Saddam Hussein	63	1979-2003
Forced Retirement	Italy	Benito Mussolini	60	1922-1943
Forced Retirement	Malawi	Hastings Kamuzu Banda	95	1966-1994
Forced Retirement	Mali	Modibo Keita	53	1960-1968
Forced Retirement	Mali	Moussa Traore	54	1968-1991
Forced Retirement	Myanmar	Ne Win	78	1962-1988
Forced Retirement	Nigeria	Yakubu Gowon	41	1966-1975
Forced Retirement	Nigeria	Ibrahim Babangida	52	1985-1993
Forced Retirement	Pakistan	Pervez Musharraf	65	2001-2008
Forced Retirement	Pakistan	Agha Muhammad Yahya Khan	54	1969-1971
Forced Retirement	Pakistan	Ayub Khan	61	1958-1969
Forced Retirement	Peru	Alberto Fujimori	62	1990-2000
Forced Retirement	Philippines	Ferdinand Marcos	69	1965-1986

Forced Retirement	Portugal	Marcelo Caetano	68	1968-1974
Forced Retirement	Romania	Ion Antonescu	62	1940-1944
Forced Retirement	Romania	King Michael	25	1940-1947
Forced Retirement	Russia	Nikita Khrushchev	70	1953-1964
Forced Retirement	Rwanda	Jean Kambanda	39 (Died in office)	1994-1994
Forced Retirement	Somalia	Mohamed Siad Barre	71	1969-1991
Forced Retirement	South Korea	Syngman Rhee	85	1948-1960
Forced Retirement	Sudan	Gaafar Nimeiry	55	1969-1985
Forced Retirement	Thailand	Plaek Phibun-songkhram	60	1938-1944, 1948-1957
Forced Retirement	Thailand	Thanom Kittikachorn	62	1963-1973
Forced Retirement	Thailand	Thaksin Shinawatra	57	2001-2006
Forced Retirement	Thailand	Chatichai Choonhavan	70	1988-1991
Forced Retirement	Tunisia	Zine El Abidine Ben Ali	74	1987-2011
Forced Retirement	Uganda	Idi Amin	53	1971-1979
Forced Retirement	Uganda	Milton Obote	46	1966-1971
Forced Retirement	Uganda	Milton Obote	60	1980-1985

Forced Retirement	Venezuela	Marcos Pérez Jiménez	44	1948-1958
Forced Retirement	Yugoslavia (1989)	Slobodan Milosevic	60	1989-2000
Forced Retirement	Zimbabwe	Robert Mugabe	93	1980-2017
Forced Retirement	Argentina	Alejandro Agustin Lanusse	54	1971-1973
Forced Retirement	Argentina	Roberto Eduardo Viola	57	March 1981-December 1981
Forced Retirement	Argentina	Leopoldo Galtieri	56	1981-1982
Forced Retirement	Brazil	Getúlio Vargas	63	1930-1945
Forced Retirement	Burundi	Jean-Baptiste Bagaza	41	1976-1987
Forced Retirement	Cambodia	Pol Pot	56	1963-1981
Killed in Office	Argentina	Pedro Eugenio Aramburu	67 (Died in office)	1955-1958
Killed in Office	Bangladesh	Ziaur Rahman	45 (Died in office)	1977-1981
Killed in Office	Burkina Faso	Thomas Sankara	37 (Died in office)	1983-1987
Killed in Office	Chad	Francois Tombalbaye	56 (Died in office)	1960-1975
Killed in Office	Egypt	Anwar Sadat	62 (Died in office)	1970-1981
Killed in Office	Germany	Adolf Hitler	56 (Died in office)	1933-1945

Killed in Office	Guatemala	Carlos Castillo Armas	43 (Died in office)	1954-1957
Killed in Office	Iraq	Abd Al-Karim Qasim	49 (Died in office)	1958-1963
Killed in Office	Nigeria	Sani Abacha	54 (Died in office)	1993-1998
Killed in Office	Nigeria	Johnson Aguiyi-Ironsi	42 (Died in office)	Jan 1966-July 1966
Killed in Office	Romania	Nicolae Ceausescu	71 (Died in office)	1965-1989
Killed in Office	Rwanda	Juvenal Habyarimana	57 (Died in office)	1973-1994
Killed in Office	South Korea	Park Chung-hee	61 (Died in office)	1963-1979
Natural Causes	Algeria	Houari Boumediene	46 (Died in office)	1965-1978
Natural Causes	Angola	Agostinho Neto	57 (Died in office)	1975-1979
Natural Causes	Brazil	Artur da Costa e Silva	69 (Died in office)	1967-1969
Natural Causes	China	Mao Zedong	82 (Died in office)	1943-1976
Natural Causes	China	Chiang Kai-shek	87 (Died in office)	1950-1975
Natural Causes	Cote d'Ivoire	Felix Houphouet-Boigny	88 (Died in office)	1960-1993
Natural Causes	Egypt	Gamal Abdel Nasser	52 (Died in office)	1956-1970
Natural Causes	Greece	Ioannis Metaxas	69 (Died in office)	1936-1941
Natural Causes	Guinea	Ahmed Sekou Toure	62 (Died in office)	1958-1984

Natural Causes	Haiti	Francois Duvalier	64 (Died in office)	1957-1971
Natural Causes	Iran	Ruhollah Khomeini	86 (Died in office)	1979-1989
Natural Causes	North Korea	Kim Il-Sung	82 (Died in office)	1948-1994
Natural Causes	North Korea	Kim Jong-Il	70 (Died in office)	1994-2011
Natural Causes	Portugal	Antonio de Oliveira Salazar	79 (Died in office)	1932-1968
Natural Causes	Russia	Josef Stalin	74 (Died in office)	1924-1953
Natural Causes	Russia	Leonid Brezhnev	75 (Died in office)	1964-1982
Natural Causes	Saudi Arabia	Abdullah bin Abdulaziz Al Saud	90 (Died in office)	2005-2015
Natural Causes	Spain	Francisco Franco	82	1936-1975
Natural Causes	Syria	Hafez al-Assad	69 (Died in office)	1971-2000
Natural Causes	Thailand	Sarit Thanarat	55 (Died in office)	1959-1963
Natural Causes	Uzbekistan	Islam Karimov	78 (Died in office)	1991-2016
Natural Causes	Venezuela	Hugo Chavez	58 (Died in office)	1999-2013
Natural Causes	Vietnam	Ho Chi-Minh	79 (Died in office)	1951-1969
Natural Causes	Yugoslavia (1989)	Tito	87 (Died in office)	1953-1980

Still in Power	Algeria	Abdelaziz Bouteflika	N/A	1999-present
Still in Power	Cambodia	Hun Sen	N/A	1984-present
Still in Power	Cameroon	Paul Biya	N/A	1982-present
Still in Power	Chad	Idriss Deby	N/A	1990-present
Still in Power	China	Xi Jinping	N/A	2012-present
Still in Power	Egypt	Abdel Fattah el-Sisi	N/A	2014-present
Still in Power	Iran	Ali Khamenei	N/A	1989-present
Still in Power	Kazakhstan	Nursultan Nazarbayev	N/A	1991-present
Still in Power	North Korea	Kim Jong-Un	N/A	2011-present
Still in Power	Philippines	Rodrigo Duterte	N/A	2016-present
Still in Power	Russia	Vladimir Putin	N/A	2000-present
Still in Power	Rwanda	Paul Kagame	N/A	2000-present
Still in Power	Sudan	Omar al-Bashir	N/A	1989-present
Still in Power	Syria	Bashar al-Assad	N/A	2000-present
Still in Power	Thailand	Prayut Chan-o-cha	N/A	2014-present
Still in Power	Turkey	Recep Tayyip Erdogan	N/A	2014-present

Still in Power	Uzbekistan	Shavkat Mirziyoyev	N/A	2016-present
Still in Power	Venezuela	Nicolas Maduro	N/A	2013-present
Voluntary Retirement	Angola	Jose Eduardo dos Santos	75	1979-2017
Voluntary Retirement	Argentina	Reynaldo Bignone	55	1982-1983
Voluntary Retirement	Argentina	Jorge Rafael Videla	55	1976-1981
Voluntary Retirement	Brazil	Emilio Garrastazu Medici	73	1969-1974
Voluntary Retirement	Brazil	Humberto de Alencar Castelo Branco	69	1964-1967
Voluntary Retirement	China	Hu Jintao	70	2002-2012
Voluntary Retirement	China	Deng Xiaoping	82	1982-1987
Voluntary Retirement	Cuba	Fidel Castro	85	1961-2011
Voluntary Retirement	Cuba	Raul Castro	86	2011-2018
Voluntary Retirement	Ghana	Jerry Rawlings	53	1981-2001
Voluntary Retirement	Kenya	Daniel arap Moi	78	1978-2002
Voluntary Retirement	Myanmar	Than Shwe	77	1992-2011
Voluntary Retirement	Nigeria	Olusegun Obasanjo	70	1976-1979

Voluntary Retirement	Peru	Manuel Odria	60	1948-1956
Voluntary Retirement	Poland	Wojciech Jaruzelski	67	1981-1990
Voluntary Retirement	Thailand	Kriangsak Chamanan	62	1977-1980
Voluntary Retirement	Thailand	Surayud Chulanot	64	2006-2008
Voluntary Retirement	Zambia	Kenneth Kaunda	67	1964-1991

APPENDIX II

A full list of treaties analyzed by the author, as well as definitions and explanations, is available online at www.afpc.org.

Date of Entry into Force for Russia	Treaty	Treaty Category	Russian violation?
1921	Treaty of Moscow (Treaty of Brotherhood)	Territorial Issues	Presumed in compliance
1928	Protocol for the Prohibition of the Use in War of Asphyxiating, Poisonous or other Gases, and of Bacteriological Methods of Warfare (Geneva Protocol)	Arms Control	In breach (as USSR)
1929	Kellogg-Briand Pact	Rules of War	In breach
1935	Svalbard Treaty	Territorial Issues	Unclear
1936	Montreux Convention Regarding the Regime of Straits	Maritime Matters	Unclear
1945	UN Charter	UN and Related Organizations	In breach

1945	Agreement relating to prisoners of war and civilians liberated by forces operating under Soviet command and forces operating under United States of America command	Rules of War	Presumed in compliance
1946	Polish-Soviet Border Agreement of August 1945	Territorial Issues	In compliance
1949	Geneva Conventions	Human Rights	In breach
1954	Convention on the Prevention and Punishment of the Crime of Genocide (Genocide Convention)	Human Rights	Presumed in compliance
1954	Convention for the Suppression of the Traffic in Persons and of the Exploitation of the Prostitution of Others	Human Rights	In breach
1963	Treaty Banning Nuclear Weapon Tests in the Atmosphere, in Outer Space and Under Water (Partial Nuclear Test Ban Treaty)	Arms Control	Presumed in breach
1964	Vienna Convention on Diplomatic Relations	Diplomatic and Consular Relations	Presumed in breach

1971	Agreement on measures to reduce the risk of outbreak of nuclear war	Nonproliferation	Presumed in compliance
1972	Treaty on the Prohibition of the Emplacement of Nuclear Weapons and Other Weapons of Mass Destruction on the Sea-Bed and the Ocean Floor and in the Subsoil thereof (Seabed Arms Control Treaty)	Arms Control	Presumed in compliance
1973	Agreement on the prevention of nuclear war	Rules of War	Unclear
1975	Convention on the Prohibition of the Development, Production and Stockpiling of Bacteriological (Biological) and Toxin Weapons and on their Destruction (Biological Weapons Convention)	Arms Control	Presumed in breach
1976	International Covenant on Civil and Political Rights (ICCPR)	Human Rights	In breach

1978	Convention on the Prohibition of Military or Any Other Hostile Use of Environmental Modification Techniques (ENMOD)	Rules of War	Presumed in compliance
1983	Convention on Certain Conventional Weapons	Arms Control	Presumed in breach
1983	International Convention concerning the Use of Broadcasting in the Cause of Peace	Telecommunication	In breach
1987	Convention on Assistance in the Case of a Nuclear Accident or Radiological Emergency	Atomic Energy	Presumed in compliance
1987	International Convention against the Taking of Hostages (Hostages Convention)	Law Enforcement	Presumed in breach
1987	Convention against Torture and Other Cruel, Inhuman or Degrading Treatment or Punishment (United Nations Convention against Torture)	Human Rights	In breach

1988	Treaty on the elimination of their intermediate-range and shorter-range missiles (INF Treaty)	Arms Control	In breach
1990	Charter of Paris for a New Europe (Paris Charter)	Diplomatic and Consular Relations	In breach
1990	Treaty on the limitation of underground nuclear weapon tests	Arms Control	Presumed in compliance
1990	Agreement on the prevention of dangerous military activities	Defense	Unclear
1990	Agreement on reciprocal advance notification of major strategic exercises	Nonproliferation	Presumed in breach
1991	Belavezha Accords	Territorial Issues	In breach
1991	1991 Sino-Soviet Border Agreement	Territorial Issues	In breach
1992	Treaty on Conventional Armed Forces in Europe	Arms Control	In breach
1993	Convention Relating to the Status of Refugees (1951 Refugee Convention)	Human Rights	In breach
1993	Protocol Relating to the Status of Refugees	Human Rights	In breach
1994	Bishkek Protocol	Occupation and Peacekeeping	Presumed in breach

1994	Budapest Memorandum on Security Assurances	Territorial Issues	In breach
1997	1997 Moscow Memorandum	Territorial Issues	In breach
1997	Convention on the Prohibition of the Development, Production, Stockpiling and Use of Chemical Weapons and on their Destruction (Chemical Weapons Convention)	Arms Control	In breach
1997	UN Convention on the Law of the Sea	Maritime Matters	In breach
1998	European Convention on Human Rights	Human Rights	In breach
1998	Framework Convention for the Protection of National Minorities	Human Rights	In breach
1999	Partition Treaty on the Status and Conditions of the Black Sea Fleet	Defense	In breach
2000	START II	Arms Control	Presumed in breach
2001	International Convention for the Suppression of Terrorist Bombings (Terrorist Bombings Convention)	Law Enforcement	Unclear

2002	International Convention for the Suppression of the Financing of Terrorism (Terrorist Financing Convention)	Law Enforcement	In breach
2003	Strategic Offensive Reductions Treaty (SORT)	Arms Control	Presumed in compliance
2004	Treaty of Amity and Cooperation in Southeast Asia	Peace	Presumed in compliance
2006	Framework Convention for the Protection of the Marine Environment of the Caspian Sea	Environment and Conservation	Presumed in compliance
2007	Council of Europe Convention on the Prevention of Terrorism	Law Enforcement	Presumed in breach
2007	International Convention for the Suppression of Acts of Nuclear Terrorism (Nuclear Terrorism Convention)	Law Enforcement	Presumed in breach
2008	Protocol on Explosive Remnants of War	Arms Control	Unclear
2011	Sino-Russian Treaty of Friendship	Defense	Unclear

2011	Agreement on the transit of armaments, military equipment, military property, and personnel through the territory of the Russian Federation in connection with the participation of the United States of America in efforts for ensuring the security, stabilization and reconstruction of the Islamic Republic of Afghanistan	Defense	Unclear
2011	Measures for Further Reduction and Limitation of Strategic Offensive Arms (New START)	Arms Control	In breach
2011	Vienna Document 2011	Defense	In breach
2013	17 December 2013 Ukrainian-Russian Action Plan	Trade and Investment	In breach
2014	Minsk	Occupation and Peacekeeping	In breach
2015	Minsk II	Occupation and Peacekeeping	In breach

INDEX

Alikhanov, Anton, 21
Amur Oblast, 43
anti-reform, 54
arable land, 43
Arendt, Hannah, 38
assassination, 30–31
Azinheira, Amanda, 7

Bakatin, Vadim, 57
Berezkin, Gregory, 24
Brezhnev, Leonid, 10, 14, 52
Bukharin, Nikolai, 49–50

Castro, Fidel, 8
Ceausescu, Nikolae, 62
censorship, 24
Central Asia, 36–38, 40–41, 45–46
chaos, in Russia, 30, 33–34, 38, 41–46
Chemezov, Sergei, 22
China, 37; arable land and, 43; chaos from, 42; migration from, 44;
    Moscow and, 34; policy with, 30, 34–36; Russian Far East and,
    34; Russia problems with, 38–39; water issues with, 42–43
color revolution, 9, 49
Communist Party: Brezhnev and, 52; movements and, 22; Politburo
    and, 10; Soviet Union and, 6; Zyuganov with, 56

coups, 9–11, 23, 31, 47; color revolution and, 49; with power
    struggles, 32; regional elites attempts of, 19; retirement and, 8
Crimea, 33
Cuba, 8
Cuban missile crisis, 51–52
cyberspace, 23–24

dictators, 7–8, 49, 62
Directorate, 14, 17
domestic economic growth, 38–41
Dyumin, Alexi, 20

Eastern Siberia, 30
elections, 29
"Essence of Time" (movement), 22
Eurasian Disunion, 41
Europe, 35–36, 39, 44

factions of power, 14, 27
Federal Agency of Government Communication and Information
    (FAPSI), 18
Federal Protection Service (FSO), 17–18
Federal Security Service (FSB), 22, 63; growth of, 18; oligarchs in,
    13; Putin and, 18–19, 57; strengthening base of, 58
Filatov, Sergei, 55
Foreign Intelligence Service (SVR), 15–16, 57, 63
From Lenin to Malenkov: the History of World Communism
    (Seton-Watson), 51
FSB. See Federal Security Service
FSO. See Federal Protection Service

Georgia, 9, 40
Germany, 37
Gorbachev, Mikhail: challengers to, 54; power struggles of, 10–11,
    53–54; reform with, 55
GRU. See Military Intelligence Directorate

individual dissent, 61–62
infrastructure, 42–43
institutions: of MVD, 17; oligarchs and, 6; power and, 13; regional

elites and, 19; religious institutions and, 61

international norms: chaos with, 44–45; domestic economic growth within, 38–41; policy and, 37; treaty compliance and, 35, 39–40

International Republican Institute (IRI), 61

Islamist, 36, 45–46

journalists, 23–25, 60, 68

Kadyrov, Ramzan, 62

Kazakhstan, 29, 38

KGB, 21, 53–55; fraternity of, 63; power with, 62; Putin and, 22, 57–58, 62

Khasbulatov, Ruslan, 22

Khodorkovsky, Mikhail, 59, 64

Khrushchev, Nikita, 5; Duma with, 10; military-assisted purge by, 51; Politburo removing, 11; power struggles of, 9–10, 50–51; Russian Army and, 14

Kolesnikov, Andrei, 27

Kotkin, Stephen, 27

Kovalchuk, Yury, 21

Kozyrev, Andrei, 33

Kremlin, 24, 61, 64

Kurginyan, Sergey, 22

Kurile Islands, 40

Lenin, Vladimir, 9, 49

Malenkov, Georgy, 51

media: power struggles and, 25–26; Putin and, 23–25, 60; threats through, 23

Medvedev, Dmitri, 28

Middle East, 41

Migration Affairs, 17

Military Intelligence Directorate (GRU), 15

Ministry of Interior Affairs (MVD), 16–17

Mobil Unit for Special Purposes (OMON), 16

Moscow, 5, 13; China and, 34; European nationalist parties and, 36; power center of, 55; for reforms, 39; violent protests in, 56; Washington, D. C. and, 14

Moskvy, Ekho, 23

movements: Communist Party and, 22; in Russia, 22, 30, 38
Muslims, 41
MVD. See Ministry of Interior Affairs

National Endowment for Democracy (NED), 61
National Guard (Rosgvardia), 16
nationalist ideology, 63
natural death, 29–30, 47
Nazarbayev, Nursultan, 38
NED. See National Endowment for Democracy
newspapers, 24–25
non-governmental organizations (NGOs), 61

oligarchs: FSB with, 13; institutions and, 6; power struggles for, 59; Putin and, 25–26; for resignation, 31–32
OMON. See Mobil Unit for Special Purposes
On Revolution (Arendt), 38

Podgorny, Nikolai, 52
policy: adjustments for, 33–36; with Central Asia, 37–38; with China, 34–36; with Europe, 35; international norms and, 37; in Russia, 5; U.S. implications of, 28–30
Politburo, 10–11, 49–53
Politkovskaya, Anna, 64
post-Soviet leaders, 54–64
post-Soviet Union, 6
power: Brezhnev struggles with, 10, 52; on centralizing, 58–59; dictators still in, 8; factions of, 14; Gorbachev struggles with, 10–11; institutions and, 13; with KGB, 62; politicians and, 21–22; Putin and, 27–30, 62–64; Putin's crowd and, 33–38; resignation and, 32; in Russia, 5; Russian leaders rise to, 9–12; short-term holders of, 53; Soviet leaders rise to, 9–12; Stalin holding, 49–50
power struggles: of Brezhnev, 52; coup with, 32; of Gorbachev, 10–11, 53–54; GRU and, 15; of Khrushchev, 9–10, 50–51; media role in, 25–26; for MVD, 17; for oligarchs, 59; for post-Soviet leaders, 54–64; Putin and, 57–64; Russian Army with, 14; Russia with, 41; for Stalin, 49–50; for Yeltsin, 54–57
private sector, 6
propaganda, 11, 23

Putin, Vladimir, 3, 6; assassination and, 30–31; FSB and, 18–19, 57; FSO for, 18; health of, 5, 7; individual dissent and, 61; KGB and, 22, 57–58, 62; killings by, 63–64; leaving power, 27–30; media and, 23–25, 60; money and, 63; National Guard and, 16; natural death of, 7, 29–30; oligarchs and, 25–26; politicians and, 20–21; power and, 8, 27–30, 62–64; power struggles and, 57–64; resignation forced on, 31–32; retirement for, 8, 27–28; Russian Orthodox Church with, 11; Sechin and, 21; Syria and, 12; on using fear, 63–64
Putin's crowd, 33–38

reforms, 33–34, 36; with Gorbachev, 55; Moscow for, 39; Russian leaders with, 47–48; societal change with, 47
regional elites, 19–20
religious institutions, 61
repression, effective, 11, 47–48
resignation, 31–32
retirement, 8, 27–28
Rogozin, Dmitry, 63
Rojavin, Alexander, 35
Romanov dynasty, 6
Rosgvardia. See National Guard
Russia: censorship in, 24; Central Asia and, 40–41; chaos in, 30, 33–34, 38, 41–46; China border with, 43–44; China problems with, 38–39; cyberspace in, 23–24; Europe and, 39; internal empire of, 35, 40, 45; in Kazakhstan, 29; Middle East and, 41; movements in, 22, 30, 38; policy in, 35–36; power in, 5; with power struggles, 41; private sector in, 6; Rosgvardia and, 16; sanctions on, 36–37; scientists in, 26; television in, 23; treaty compliance, 35, 37, 39–40, 44–45
Russian Army: Brezhnev and, 14; command of, 13–15; Directorate within, 14; interest to, 14–15; power struggles in, 14; Spetsnaz troops in, 15
Russian education, 60
Russian Far East, 30, 34
Russian leaders: changes with, 48; effective repression from, 47–48; power rise of, 9–12; with reforms, 47–48; U.S. and, 47–48, 51
Russian Orthodox Church, 11

sanctions, 31, 33, 35–37

Sechin, Igor, 21
self-censorship, 24
Semenov, Vladimir, 43
Seton-Watson, Hugh, 51
Shelepin, Alexander, 52
Shoigu, Sergey, 22
Shucheng, Wang, 42
SOBR. See Special Unit for Quick Reaction
Sobyanin, Sergei, 20
Soviet Union: Communist Party and, 6; Kurile Islands and, 40;
    leaders power rise of, 9–12. See also Russia
Special Unit for Quick Reaction (SOBR), 16
Spetsnaz troops, 15
spies, 15
Stalin, Joseph, 9; death of, 50; holding power, 49–50; power
    struggles for, 49–50; repression used by, 11
Suslov, Mikhail, 10, 53
SVR. See Foreign Intelligence Service
Syria, 12, 22, 32–33

television, 23
Tkachev, Alexander, 42
treaty compliance: chaos with, 44–45; international norms and, 35,
    39–40; policy and, 37
Trotsky, Leon, 49–50
Turchak, Andrei, 20–21

Ukraine, 9, 33, 40
United States (U.S.): Khrushchev and, 51; policy implications for,
    28–30; Russian leaders and, 47–48, 51
USSR (Union of Soviet Socialist Republics). See Soviet Union

Virtual Private Networks (VPNs), 24
VPNs. See Virtual Private Networks

Washington, D. C., 14, 35
water issues,with china, 42–43
We Will Reclaim Russia for Ourselves (Rogozin), 63
WHO. See World Health Organization
World Health Organization (WHO), 7

World War II, 40, 45, 50

Yeltsin, Boris, 6, 14, 54; Gorbachev and, 54; Kurginyan against, 22; on leaving power, 28; oligarchs and, 59; opposition to, 55–56; power struggles for, 54–57; Putin and, 57

Zdanovich, Alexander, 60
Zhukov, Marshall, 10
Zinoviev, Grigory, 49–50
Zolotov, Viktor, 16
Zyuganov, Gennady, 56

CPSIA information can be obtained
at www.ICGtesting.com
Printed in the USA
LVHW080107310519
619695LV00006B/51/P